The Story Behind…
Too Much Punch For Judy

By Mark Wheeller

Design & Layout by Barrie Sapsford

Pping Publishng
Southampton UK
wheellerplays.com

Published by: Pping Publishing
Southampton
www.wheellerplays.com

© Mark Wheeller 2013/2017
Second Edition 2017

Cover Artwork by: Steve Crisp - © Barrie Sapsford 2013
Illustrations © Midas Marketing 2013

The moral right of Mark Wheeller to be identified as the author of this work has been asserted by him in accordance with the Copyright, Designs and Patents Act 1988.

All rights reserved. Except as permitted under current legislation, no part of this work may be photocopied, storied in a retrieval system, published, performed in public, adapted, broadcast, transmitted, recorded or reproduced in any form or by any means, without the prior permission of the copyright owners. Enquiries should me made to Wheellerplays@gmail.com

The Story Behind – *Too Much Punch For Judy* by Mark Wheeller

British Library Cataloguing in Publication Data. A catalogue record for this book is available from the British Library

ISBN: 978-0-9575659-4-4

Printed by Book Printing UK
Remus House, Coltsfoot Drive, Peterborough PE2 9BF

The Story Behind - Too Much Punch For Judy by Mark Wheeller

Acknowledgments

Rachael Wheeller: The great woman behind the barely adequate man.
All the sources for kind permission to use their words.
Toni and Vi, her mother;
PC's Abrahams and Caten;
Sister Hunt;
Duncan Wick.
Roy Nevitt and Stantonbury Campus Theatre for introducing me to Documentary Theatre.
Mick and Sylvia Baker for their initial inspiration and their tremendous support throughout the EYT performances.
The performers in the Epping Youth Theatre productions Quenchers (1986) and Too Much Punch For Judy (1987):- Kim Baker; Fay Davies; Jo Dumelow; Paul Elliott; Ryan Gilbey; George Griffiths; Emma Jefferson; Debbie Mitchell; Debbie Pollard; Jo Redman; John Rowley; Barrie Sapsford; Beth Spendlow; Emma Turner; Anna Wallbank and Jon Ward.
CADD (Campaign Against Drinking and Driving) for their tremendous campaign. Derek Rutherford, Institute of Alcohol Studies.
David Lyndsay & Rosie Welch (of Essex County Council Highways Department; Frank Nunneley (Hertfordshire County Council - Road Safety) and Road Safety Officers in England, Scotland and Wales who have offered their support to the play's continued success.
Helen & Phil Lowe and Touchstone Theatre Company for the first professional production.
Mat Kane, Antony Audenshaw and Yvonne Allen, and Ape Theatre Company for their stunning performances since 1988 in England, Cyprus, Germany, Jersey.
Mat, Steve, Fay, and Tor for their contribution to the first Ape production which inspired the opening and closing scenes. Alistair Black, Hampshire County Council Drama Inspector, for the idea to re-visit the beginning of the play at the end... nice one!
Meg Davis & Sophie Gorell Barnes and MBA Literary Agency for continued belief.
Dawn Boyfield, Evie Efthimiou and Lynda Taylor from dbda.
Yvonne Allen, Kat Chivers, Jo Dalton, Fay Davies, Cris Lewis, Roy Nevitt, Olivia Prince, Tommy Scotting, Jack Simmonds, Rachael Wheeller for their various read throughs and help in developing this book.
Matt Allen, Tony Audenshaw, Jo Dalton, Fay Davies, Ben O'Shea, John Rowley, Steve North, Charlie Wheeller, for their contributions. Barrie Sapsford for his design ideas.

Photographs/Images: Cover: Barrie Sapsford

Page 5, 165-167 & back cover: Original Police photo with thanks to Essex Police.
Page 33: Picture of Jo and Toni from family collection.
Page 46: Department of Transport for Northern Ireland Road Safety poster.
Page 50, 64, 78 & 90: Epping Youth Theatre photographs.
Page 15, 16, 19, 28, 34, 56, 68, 80, 84, 127, 150 & 152: Mark Wheeller's personal collection Page 34, 57 & 112: Photo & Image design by John Rowley
Page 128: Ape Theatre Company Photographs by Derek Jones
Page 142 Tufty: Kind permission of RoSPA
Page 130 Chicken: Oldham Road Safety Unit
Page 164: Callum Watts
Page 175: Fay Davies
Page 177: Rachael Wheeller - (Authors Picture)
Page 178: Zoe Sapsford
Page 180: Chris Webb/Danny Sturrock

The Story Behind - Too Much Punch For Judy by Mark Wheeller

Contents: **Page**

Preface – Setting the Scene	5
1. Context – (Nick, and those studying the play. This is the Chapter you really ought to read!)	10
2. Too Much Punch For Judy – The research	35
3. Quenchers – Preparations	41
4. Quenchers – First Performances	70
5. Quenchers – On the Edinburgh Fringe	79
6. Too Much Punch For Judy - EYT rehearsals	86
7. Too Much Punch For Judy – First Performances and the NSDF	98
8. Too Much Punch For Judy – Enter the Professionals	113
9. Too Much Punch For Judy – Stranger than Fiction	131
10. Too Much Punch For Judy – Family Tree	141
11. Too Much Punch For Judy – Back to School	145
Appendix 1. Staging The Accident	152
Afterthought. Too Much Punch for Judy – Revisited	161
Appendix 2. Essex Police Accident Photographs	165
Postscript to the second Edition:	168

The Story Behind - Too Much Punch For Judy by Mark Wheeller

Preface

May 20th 1983:

A lonely road near Epping.

A Renault 5 car comes off the road and hits a bridge.

The scaffolding construction slices through the car windscreen.

The driver, Judy, escapes unhurt but the passenger, her sister Joanna, is killed outright. Jo and Judy had both been drinking.

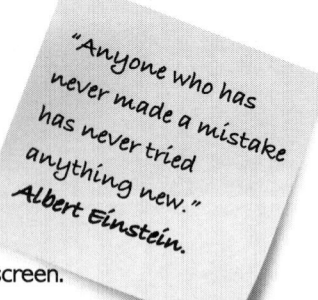

"Anyone who has never made a mistake has never tried anything new."
Albert Einstein.

In 1985 I was the Director of Epping Youth Theatre and had completed one successful documentary play *Race to Be Seen*. I was keen to develop another and took on a (part documentary) play exploring alcohol misuse to be called *Quenchers*. I thought it was complete when I saw the Christmas 1985 Drink Drive campaign featuring the newly formed UK Campaign Against Drinking and Driving (CADD). I was frustrated that I had not previously thought about this topic. It was important and potent... too potent for me to ignore.

I went on to meet "Judy" (real name Toni) who willingly told me her tragic story. I interviewed her, her mother, the first person to arrive on the scene of the accident, the policemen who attended and the nurse who dealt with Judy when she arrived in the hospital. All had vivid memories of the incident and, using their words, I constructed a scene that became the end to *Quenchers*. It was clear to me that this tragic story deserved more than just a fifteen-minute epilogue. *Too Much Punch For Judy* was born the following year.

The Story Behind - Too Much Punch For Judy by Mark Wheeller

Too Much Punch For Judy

* Written between 1985 and 1987

* Is one of, or perhaps even the, most performed contemporary play(s) ever (I would love to know where it ranks)

* Has sold 33,936 scripts to date (November 2017) worldwide

* Has been performed 6020 times to date (November 2017) [1]

* Has been seen by at least half a million people in licensed performances. Given an average audience of 150, it may be nearer one million (902,400)

* Has toured, predominantly by Ape Theatre Company, secondary schools across the UK (Autumn and Spring terms) every years since 1987

* Is an established exam performance study script for GCSE, Btec, A'Level, University and Drama School students

Messages from students who study the play sparked my initial inspiration to write this book. The email that follows, arrived the day I started on it. This is not dramatic licence; like everything in this book… it actually happened:

---

[1] These statistics only include "public" or professional performances that require permission from me. I am well aware that it has been performed for exams (where no invited audience attends) many more times without my knowledge.

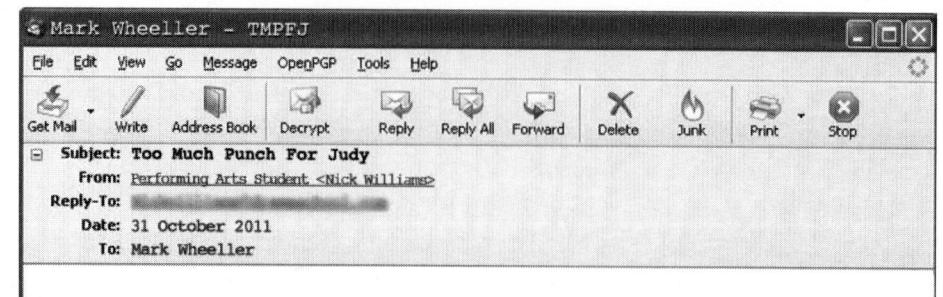

The Story Behind - Too Much Punch For Judy by Mark Wheeller

> **Subject:** Too Much Punch For Judy
> **From:** Performing Arts Student <Nick Williams>
> **Reply-To:** ████████████
> **Date:** 31 October 2011
> **To:** Mark Wheeller
>
> 31st October 2011
>
> Hi, I'm currently studying Performing Arts at A-Level. After reading the first couple of pages of Too Much Punch for Judy, I fell in love with it. It's been written with so much thought and effort. I can't wait to read the next one. As part of my course we have to produce a showcase, which includes two solo pieces and a duologue. For one of my solo pieces I am performing Duncan's monologue.
>
> I need to produce a working log, which explains the context of the play and the social and historical influences to the examiner. I would really appreciate it if you could send me some information to help me. I know it is based on true events of a car crash, but is there anything else that influenced you to write this documentary drama?
>
> If you could reply, that would be truly helpful.
>
> Thank You
> Nick Williams

I hope this book will not only answer Nick's question but will also shed some light on the hidden process of creating a play.

I am sorry this was too late for your project Nick, but I hope you did well!

The Story Behind - Too Much Punch For Judy by Mark Wheeller

Now, for those wanting some historical context, here are ten top facts about that era... and if you don't, please skip to the next section!

TOP 10 FACTS

TOP 10 HISTORICAL FACTS FROM THE ERA

1. THATCHER 3RD TERM
Margaret Thatcher was voted in for her third term as UK Prime Minister. I confess I voted for her (first term) on the basis that as the first woman to gain that position she would be more determined to do the job well. By the time this election came around I didn't!

2. HOUSE PRICES TO RISE
Average house price was £44,000; pretty much what I paid for mine back then.

3. PETROL HITS RECORD HIGH
A gallon of petrol was £1.89 – I had a blue Renault 4 at this time.

4. TERRY WAITE KIDNAPPED!
Terry Waite the special envoy of the Archbishop of Canterbury was kidnapped in Lebanon – I remember this on the news vividly.

5. HUNGERFORD MASSACRE
Michael Ryan killed 16 people in Hungerford and then committed suicide – and whenever I travel through Hungerford I think of that tragedy.

6. FISH IN HOT WATER!
Great British Storm famously not predicted by Michael Fish on the BBC – that night we took in a little cat that we called Pussing. She was homeless and sheltering from the storm and meowing very loudly!

7. Z88 HITS THE SHELVES
Clive Sinclair launched the Z88 portable computer. At that point I had barely even seen a computer, let alone owned one.

8. DISPOSABLE CONTACTS
Disposable contact lenses became available for commercial distribution – I wore hard contact lenses at the time... they hurt at first but I became accustomed to them.

9. HOME RUN FOR HOMER!
The Simpsons are seen on the TV for the first time – I remember the excitement of my Youth Theatre when we visited the USA a few years later at seeing this series for the first time.

10. KARAOKE HAS ARRIVED!
Karaoke was invented – I'd love this but don't have the nerve to do it. I must!!!

The Story Behind - Too Much Punch For Judy by Mark Wheeller

1987 Theatreboard
THE WORLD OF MUSIC AND THEATRE
Top 3 from the Theatre World

1: Director of the Year was Declan Donnellan. He also has the accolade of being the first director I'd seen approaching Shakespeare (with his company Cheek By Jowl) in an imaginative manner which I loved! I saw his 1987 production of **Macbeth**.

2: Serious Money by Carly Churchill won the Olivier Award for best play of the year. I've never seen this.

3: Teechers by John Godber was premiered at the Edinburgh Festival Fringe - I've seen this more times than I care to remember and wish I'd written it.

For me, on a personal note, in 1987 there were five key markers:

1. Epping Youth Theatre performed **Too Much Punch For Judy**. By the end of the year a professional theatre company had toured secondary schools in Essex and throughout Scotland. I had become a "professional" writer!

2. David Bowie released a new album **Never Let Me Down** and undertook his Glass Spider tour, which I saw in July. Most years are marked, for me, with David Bowie events.

3. I left Epping Youth Theatre and St John's School Epping.

4. I became Head of Drama at Oaklands, in Southampton where I was to run OYT (Oaklands Youth Theatre later Oasis Youth Theatre. I arrived at the interview with the freshly released David Bowie song, 'Day In Day Out' blasting out of my cassette player. That song always reminds me of that day and I always play it at the start of every school year. I was given an Amstrad green screen word processor to write my plays. I was very excited to have such an amazing piece of technology... only one problem... I couldn't type... a major hurdle to overcome.

5. On my first day at Oaklands I met my future wife, Rachael, without doubt, the best thing to have happened to me.

The Story Behind - Too Much Punch For Judy by Mark Wheeller

Context:
(Nick, and those studying the play. This is the chapter you really ought to read!)

> "When you grow up, you tend to get told the world is the way it is and your life is just to live inside the world. Try not to bash into the walls too much. Try to have a nice family life, have fun, save a little money. That's a very limited life. Life can be broader once you discover one simple fact:
>
> Everything around you that you call life was made up by people that were no smarter than you and you can change it, you can influence it. You can build your own things that other people can use. Once you learn that you'll never be the same again!"
>
> Steve Jobs (Apple) 1994

In this chapter I will, not only show the vacuum of my theatrical knowledge, but also show how I (we) were willing to adapt ideas we stumbled across to illustrate the context from which *Too Much Punch For Judy* emerged.

I hope this may offer others with no real knowledge or experience the realisation that they can also make exciting new work. All things are possible with determination and an ability to sift useful ideas that you chance upon at various points in your life.

Too Much Punch For Judy was not the result of some clever master plan. It grew out of another play entirely and was the result of commitment, and an enthusiasm to create captivating theatre rather than any formal academic theatre background.

To assist me in writing this book, I have looked through my production diary for the original production. I wrote these for my first three documentary plays to record the process and create a road map for future projects. I couldn't have had much of a life back then to afford the time to do such a thing; or perhaps this was my life?

Reading it has been interesting and revealing. I hadn't realised its humble beginnings.

* We failed to fill our 35-seat capacity, newly converted Drama Studio, having only 15 in the audience for the first performance

The Story Behind - Too Much Punch For Judy by Mark Wheeller

The diaries also reminded me of how inexperienced I was when I started this project with my young team from the Epping Youth Theatre. Many examples crop up in my diary but this one stands out as an illustration of our theatrical naivety:

> **Diary**
>
> 29 April 1986
>
> Today's rehearsal lived up to and beyond, my expectations! I was determined to experiment with levels, following our workshop (Adrian Phillips from Webbe Foote Theatre Company) aiming to develop our "flat" work. Paul Elliott (17) thought any use of levels would imply heavy symbolism, which he didn't want.
>
> I was relieved when John Rowley (19) supported my enthusiasm about incorporating them. John carried the group with him and soon Paul became willing to experiment.
>
> The raised areas became the source of numerous puns and jokes but improved our presentation of the scene. I cannot imagine how it could have been achieved as effectively on the flat.

Nowadays use of levels is a prerequisite for my Key Stage 3 students (11-14 year olds), but from what I say here, up until this production, I had never previously encountered them. I think this theatrical innocence would become an advantage in creating *Too Much Punch*, as we weren't beholden to any restrictive sets of guiding principles. Having said that, it could have proved a recipe for disaster.

The Story Behind - Too Much Punch For Judy by Mark Wheeller

Making plays is a journey and *Too Much Punch* was a key part of mine, which continues to this day. I learnt a lot, not by being told or reading what others had done, but by a determination to get this "show on the road," trusting that in developing our ideas, necessity would be "the mother of invention".

My background in Theatre

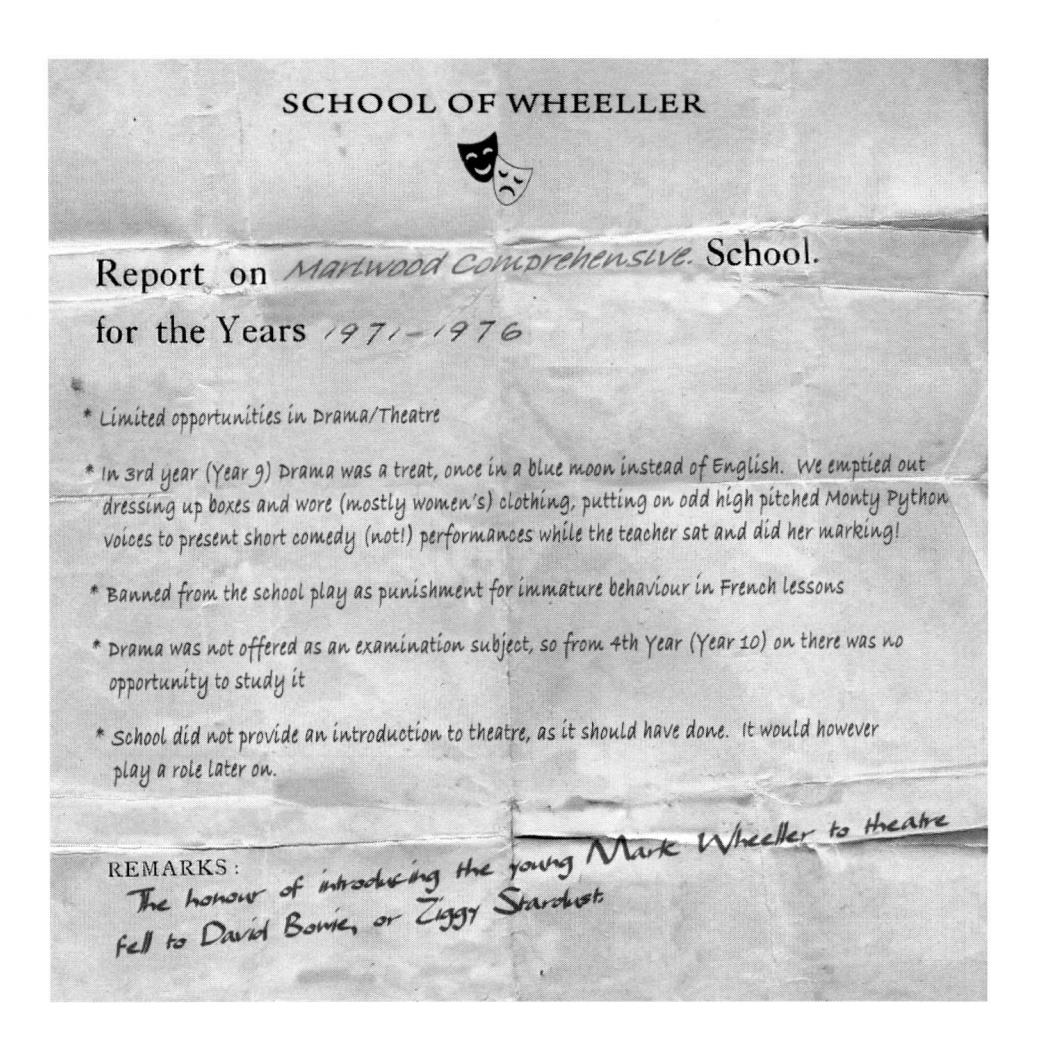

SCHOOL OF WHEELLER

Report on *Marlwood Comprehensive* School.

for the Years *1971-1976*

* Limited opportunities in Drama/Theatre

* In 3rd year (Year 9) Drama was a treat, once in a blue moon instead of English. We emptied out dressing up boxes and wore (mostly women's) clothing, putting on odd high pitched Monty Python voices to present short comedy (not!) performances while the teacher sat and did her marking!

* Banned from the school play as punishment for immature behaviour in French lessons

* Drama was not offered as an examination subject, so from 4th Year (Year 10) on there was no opportunity to study it

* School did not provide an introduction to theatre, as it should have done. It would however play a role later on.

REMARKS: The honour of introducing the young Mark Wheeller to theatre fell to David Bowie, or Ziggy Stardust.

The Story Behind - Too Much Punch For Judy by Mark Wheeller

I want to be Ziggy Stardust !!!

* *Top of the Pops* June 1972 (3rd Year/Year 9). I was watching and was transported to another exciting world. David Bowie appeared performing his new single *Starman*, dressed as alien cosmic rocker *Ziggy Stardust*. I was mesmerised and instantly became a fan. Although I (think) I realised he was merely playing the part, Bowie and Ziggy merged in my mind. I cannot explain how I viewed him other than to say I genuinely believed him (or was it Ziggy?) to be superhuman

* I bought *The Rise and Fall of Ziggy Stardust and the Spiders from Mars* album, my first, on the strength of that one performance. I couldn't see him on TV Music channels repeatedly; there weren't any, which added to the elusive and mysterious image, which the album cover also captured perfectly. I bought into it completely

* Tickets went on sale for the live *Ziggy* show in nearby Bristol. I asked my mum and dad if I could go, fully expecting them to say no

* They said yes!!! I managed to secure one ticket for £1.50. By chance a boy from my school had also done the same. His ticket unbelievably was next to mine. We went together. I can't remember his name but I remember the evening vividly!

* *Nationwide* a current affairs programme on BBC I showed a feature the week before I was due to see him, a rare opportunity to see moving pictures of him. He was also interviewed, briefly, in full Ziggy regalia. Was this Ziggy or David Bowie? I enjoyed the frisson of there being no clear delineation between reality and fiction. I didn't realise this at the time but Bowie had extended the theatrical boundaries of his show and the Ziggy Stardust character well beyond the concert itself

* June 1973: I experienced what I refer to as the "magic of theatre" for the first time as David Bowie/Ziggy Stardust appeared on stage before my eyes. People of my age were all around me screaming and fainting. I realise now it was hysteria but at the time it seemed like a spell. I knew this was David Bowie but I "suspended my disbelief" and without understanding the process, Bowie became "Ziggy." Something that was not true became "real". It was magical. I wanted to conjure this magic. Bowie had created a "plastic rock star" that was consciously faked. He made Ziggy important by hyping him. Before he (or Ziggy) was famous he employed bodyguards to escort him (or was it Ziggy?) to and from concerts, interviews etc. His way of making something seem more important than it actually was is something I took on board subconsciously and employed, albeit in a very different way, in my work

The Story Behind - Too Much Punch For Judy by Mark Wheeller

* Putting the "magic" incorrectly down to the music, rather than words, image or theatre that contextualised it, I decided I would become a tunesmith. I convinced a cleverer lad than me (Simon Guppy) in the top stream of my year to write lyrics for me, as I couldn't be bothered.[1a] I had limited ability on the piano and could sing (I had been a cathedral choirboy!) I had no idea how to write a song. Nevertheless I wrote music for Simon's lyrics.

* ## *The songs were dreadful !*

* I bought *Teach Yourself Songwriting by Martin Lindsay,* read it and despite it having been written back in 1955, gradually my songs improved (to an extent)

Hazard!

* I offered to sing in a local group; the deal was that I would honour them with my frontman aura as long as they would perform three of my songs in their set

* This arrangement lasted for two gigs, after which it became obvious to them that no one wanted to hear my songs and I wasn't keen on singing the covers they wanted me to perform. (Having said this, my perception was that no one seemed to want to listen to any of the songs as they talked through all of them, so it was difficult to judge the merits of mine as opposed to the covers.)

My attempts to be the next Ziggy Stardust had failed at the first hurdle.

I needed a plan B !

(1a) Yesterday, looking through some old folders, I discovered I did write lyrics. My memory is that I always palmed these off onto other people. Seeing them, I realise the truth is that I became fed up of waiting for them to be delivered and just got on and did them myself. I never attached any significance to them. They were a chore. That said, they serve their purpose well and indicate a bizarre, perhaps surreal, inclination.

The Story Behind - Too Much Punch For Judy by Mark Wheeller

The idea for plan B arose from my low level involvement in the local amateur theatre scene. My dad was the Musical Director for the Thornbury Amateur Operatic Society (TAOS). He invited me to become involved purely to give me something to do, as I seemed to be showing no interest in anything other than sitting upstairs writing songs. I did it to please him more than any desire to be part of this group.

* Aged 14: "Call boy". No, not what you're thinking! This involved running to dressing rooms to ensure performers arrive on stage on time calling the performers to the stage

* Aged 16: "Dancer" (not a great one) in *The Pajama Game;* also sang one line… well. (This boy has a future – I thought!)

* Aged 17: Small role in *Aladdin* pantomime (one page of alternate lines) and a solo song.

Thornbury Operatic

Mark (the dancer!) is the 3rd from the left.

The Story Behind - Too Much Punch For Judy by Mark Wheeller

Theatre was proving to be:

* Something I could do; demonstrated by lightning progress I made from Call Boy to subsidiary role in local pantomime

* A far more reliable way to get an audience to listen. They sat in rows that were difficult to escape from and weren't all chatting/shouting/throwing stuff while we were performing. None were getting drunk!

* My path to fame? I worked in a local supermarket and people started to recognise me from TAOS productions…occasionally

* A potential way of earning money rather than having to "work"

All of the above gave birth to my motivation. In reality it was actually laziness. I became motivated to do this to avoid what I saw as "work".

The combination of my experience in TAOS and there being no drama teacher at my school created my plan B:

* I formed an out of school theatre company (grand title for what it was) to present my home-grown musicals. These were little more than an opportunity for me to have my music performed. I had no interest whatsoever in writing the scripts, which, like lyrics, I viewed as "work" and of secondary importance to the music. I managed to talk various more intelligent friends (and girlfriend!) into writing them for me.

The Story Behind - Too Much Punch For Judy by Mark Wheeller

* There was a problem: To have these musicals performed, someone had to organise them, otherwise they wouldn't happen

ME!

* I appointed myself as the Artistic Director

* July 1975: *Hardened Criminals* - with a cast of less than ten

* December 1975: *Snow White* – with a cast of about 30

* March 1976: *Pierrot* – with a cast of over 70.

With respect to my writing, there was nothing here to indicate what was to come. I wasn't writing the script and as a director, no style was emerging. I was merely gaining experience and confidence by trial and error.

I had three shows under my belt when I left school. Writing and presenting my own Musical Theatre productions was, I felt, an appropriate qualification (in the absence of any others) to apply to be a Drama teacher.

To my tutor's surprise (he actually said to me "Their standards must have gone down") I was given an unconditional offer (which meant I didn't need to get any A' Levels – which I didn't) by Goldsmiths' College to do the Certificate in Education Teacher Training course with Drama as my specialist subject.

I was hired to work at the local summer holiday play scheme.

Guess what I did?

Yes. I wrote a musical (another friend wrote the script for me) and spent my summer holiday (paid!) directing that. My first professional engagement! It beat working in the local supermarket!

The Story Behind - Too Much Punch For Judy by Mark Wheeller

I was expected to study Drama "at my own level". It was assumed "my own level" was:

* To study Greek Theatre (Sophocles - *Oedipus*) and Shakespeare *(Hamlet)*

I was disappointed to discover that:

* Staging my own musicals did not feature on the college curriculum whatsoever.

I used the word "study" but "glossing over" would be a more accurate description of what I did.

This course introduced me to something that perhaps becomes the first indicator of what was to come, in terms of myself as a writer and featured, albeit in an entirely different way, in my documentary plays such as *Too Much Punch*.

* I remember being fascinated by Pinter's intention to make his characters use "truthful" language and "natural" pauses; a world away from the musicals I had experienced

* For the first time I saw "craft" in the construction of scripts

* We looked at his early work: *The Dumb Waiter, The Room* and *The Birthday Party*. Until this point I had never considered writing plays to be something I could or would ever want to do

* I was disappointed when I went to see a production of Pinter's latest production, Betrayal, at the National Theatre. I found it inaccessible and not "real' at all! (In 2017 I went to see Betrayal at the Salisbury Playhouse and loved it. I think I must have finally grown up!)

My exposure to Pinter sowed two important seeds:

* If characters are believable on stage, the words they say must be as "real" as possible

* Theatre must engage.

The Story Behind - Too Much Punch For Judy by Mark Wheeller

In my final year of the course, I was given the task of finding a short scene for two people, which I had to direct. I went to our local library and spent an afternoon searching through their tired looking plays. After about three hours I gave up and just took a play with two characters that was about the right length. This frustrating afternoon taught me another crucial lesson.

* If I create my own play, I will save myself the bother and time, of this fruitless and potentially endless search.

Once again, my innate laziness brought about my need to be creative!

My Drama studies at College were soon relegated to the background when I was offered the opportunity to become the songwriter and Musical Director for the 4R Community Dance and Drama group in nearby Lewisham.

This experience enabled me to pursue my goal of becoming a famous musical theatre composer and was, I felt, more relevant to my career aspirations: someone who organises school productions and teaches drama as a subsidiary role.

Although my involvement in 4R led to no qualification, I worked hard (obsessively) with them and learnt invaluable "directing" skills from their inspirational director Tony Key.

Tony Key directing *Beyond the Rainbow*- 4R

The Story Behind - Too Much Punch For Judy by Mark Wheeller

* A skilled facilitator working with large (100+) casts of inexperienced and non-auditioned cast members aged from 4-70+

* Didn't merely tell his cast where to stand on stage but enabled them to shape their own ideas and colour in his outline

How Tony Key hyped 4R's productions:

* Offered a template for projects such as Too Much Punch that I "curate". I choose that word quite consciously over "create"
* Tony, like David Bowie, hyped his work making it seem more important than possibly it was.

* He booked the massive (1000+ seater) Lewisham Concert Hall (where once Ziggy had performed) for a week long run

* He commissioned professional posters some of which were billboard size!

* He borrowed set and costumes from Pinewood Studios

* He invited contemporary TV stars to perform as guests in the productions

* He created such interest in his work that for example BBC2 *Horizon* filmed a documentary about 4R. To my knowledge it was never aired. I even wonder if it was all a set up to make it seem as though it was happening!

Tony was a massive influence on me and proved that one key to motivating your cast was to make what you were doing seem special, unique, just as David Bowie had done with Ziggy; simple hype! I would put that to immediate use, as I became a teacher.

My first Drama teaching job was at Stantonbury Campus in Milton Keynes, which was, at that time, considered a very progressive comprehensive school. Unusually for an English secondary school, it had a team of five (yes five!) Drama teachers and I was very much the baby, being only 21 years old.

I continued to present self-written musicals with the Stantonbury Youth Theatre. We recorded the original songs professionally as we were the "Original Cast" and produced professional looking/sounding cassettes to sell after the performance. Remembering David/Ziggy and Tony, I made much of that and raised the perception of the production.

The Story Behind - Too Much Punch For Judy by Mark Wheeller

In my second year at Stantonbury, I found myself with no one to write the script for me. I was forced to find a way of doing so myself.

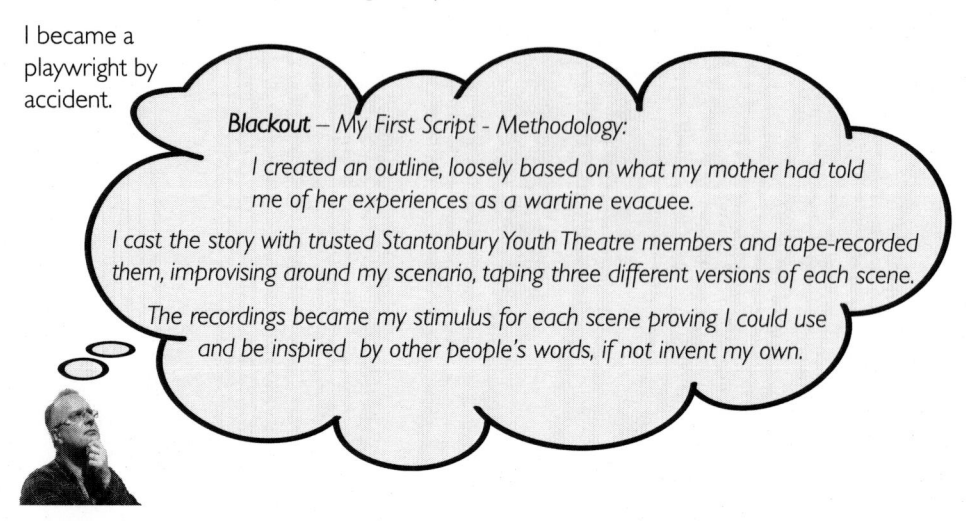

I became a playwright by accident.

Blackout – My First Script - Methodology:

I created an outline, loosely based on what my mother had told me of her experiences as a wartime evacuee.

I cast the story with trusted Stantonbury Youth Theatre members and tape-recorded them, improvising around my scenario, taping three different versions of each scene.

The recordings became my stimulus for each scene proving I could use and be inspired by other people's words, if not invent my own.

The creation of **Punch** bore much similarity to this process of using transcriptions, the main difference being that the improvisations were already in dialogue form. There were no long narrative passages in the improvised work.

I was fortunate to fall under the influence of experienced practitioners at Stantonbury. Of the four other drama teachers there, two were leaders in their respective fields. One of these was *Roy Nevitt* [2]

The Director of Drama, was a pioneer of documentary theatre. He used it in the seemingly rootless new city of Milton Keynes, as a way of developing effective community theatre with and for the local community. Before I saw his plays I pre-judged them to be academic purely because Roy was an Oxford graduate and taught A' Level Theatre which I knew I could never do! I imagined, like *Betrayal*, documentary plays would be too difficult for me to understand.

Had I looked beneath the surface of this off-putting name, documentary theatre, I would have discovered how wrong I was. This was very much theatre of the "people".

Peter Cheeseman, from the Victoria Theatre, Stoke on Trent, I later discovered, had been a major influence on Roy's work. He conceived that:

* Repertory Theatre should be like the local football team. The community know the actors by name

* The stories they tell should derive from the community

---

[2] Later to become more widely known for his work with *The Living Archive Project* in Milton Keynes.

The Story Behind - Too Much Punch For Judy by Mark Wheeller

* He was strict about using only the words spoken in interviews or found in transcripts/letters etc. The people he interviewed were "normal" people. The language they used was real and accessible
* Although songs were included in this form, it brought content to the fore, rather than existing merely to serve the songs

> "The spearhead of all our work at Stoke is the Documentary. Our writers lead the research and uncover the documents and memories on which the shows are based. My hope was that these shows would really intensify our relationship with the district and give this relationship a concrete form on the stage. They have done."
>
> *Peter Cheeseman – Director*
> *Victoria Theatre Stoke on Trent*

Documentary Plays:

* Are composed directly from primary source materials. These could include documents, minutes of meetings, letters, records of court proceedings, etc

* Bring social issues to the stage focusing on factual information

* Peter Cheeseman at the Victoria Theatre Stoke on Trent pioneered the use of Documentary Theatre. His plays used exclusively the words spoken in interviews or found in transcripts/letters etc. to become the utterance of the performer on stage

* Many people since have jumped on the documentary bandwagon, including David Hare. Nicholas Kent at the Tricycle Theatre has also made a series of Tribunal plays, based on dramatic verbatim reconstructions of public inquiries

* Documentary theatre has existed as a genre for as long as theatre itself. In 492 BC the ancient Greek playwright Phrynichus produced ***The Capture of Miletus*** about the Persian War

* ***The Laramie Project***, telling the story of the kidnap and murder of Matthew Shepard is a fascinating documentary play. The thoughts and opinions of the writers/actors/interviewees became part of the script and in the original production they played themselves saying their own words

* A recent attempt to take the form forward was a play *(Where Have I Been All My Life?)* by Alecky Blythe, produced in 2012 at the New Victoria Theatre in Newcastle-under-Lyme. The actors were told not to learn the lines, which had been selected verbatim from the people whose stories were told, but instead to hear them in their earpieces and speak them with exact attention to details of sound, volume, accent, timing and including all hesitations etc. at the moment of performance

The Story Behind - Too Much Punch For Judy by Mark Wheeller

* Alecky Blythe has also had a hit with **London Road,** a (2011) Documentary Musical, documenting the events of autumn 2006, when the life of the quiet town of Ipswich was shattered by the discovery of the bodies of five women. Adam Cork's music uses the melodic speech patterns captured on Alecky Blythe's extensive recorded interviews with the Ipswich people to create the score.

Too Much Punch, I have learnt in the research for this book, is a sub-genre of documentary theatre, called Verbatim Theatre. (Laramie and London Road are also Verbatim Theatre productions.)

Verbatim Theatre:

* Limited to making dialogue and other forms of dramatic text from the recorded voices of people speaking within or about a particular event.

The first documentary play I saw was Roy Nevitt's production of *Your Loving Brother Albert.* This was based on the letters from an underage World War I soldier in the trenches to his siblings, which were discovered many years later. I realised my prejudice about this form of theatre was unfounded. My decision to attend this, in 1980, changed my practice.

Your Loving Brother Albert.

* I was constantly aware (if only in the back of my mind) that the words in the script were "real", all direct quotes from Albert French's letters

* While watching the production I found myself imagining the real Albert writing them. This image would then fade and the theatrical reconstruction replaced it centre-stage in my mind

* I was internally cutting from one focus to another, which helped my flighty mind to maintain concentration

* This was more "real" than any invented script could ever be, even Pinter's

* Using real words from real people/letters added weight and depth to the words.

The Story Behind - Too Much Punch For Judy by Mark Wheeller

I remember thinking, after I saw that first production that I was too timid to do a documentary play on Roy's patch, but, when I left Stantonbury, I would develop my own documentary plays… and put my own spin on them. Roy's were historical stories; mine would be contemporary.

In 1982 I became the Head of Drama at St. John's School in Epping and took the opportunity to experiment with developing my own DocumentaryTheatre. **Punch** represented the culmination of my work in Epping.

My first production at St John's was a new documentary version of **Blackout**, [2a] the musical I had written for SYT.

* I incorporated interviews I conducted with four evacuees from the Epping area

* These accounts mirrored the action of the story

* No attempt was made to integrate them into the script. They were four separate characters. The actors, in modern dress delivered their lines as reminiscences from the side of stage

* This provided an opportunity for me to experiment with oral testimony in the safety of an already proven success

* The words added authenticity to the production giving it a substance that none of my previous work had ever achieved.

The Times Educational Supplement, who reviewed it, had this to say:

"The evocation of the period was so good that I spent the first act waiting for Vera Lynn's entrance."

Hugh David

[2a] Blackout can now be seen in full on YouTube

The Story Behind - Too Much Punch For Judy by Mark Wheeller

> These narrative passages highlighted a power, which I have been struggling to convey in this chapter. Today something happened which suddenly clarified why these accounts are so powerful and make it seem like we have witnessed the event itself. I realised that much of our life experience does not actually happen to us but arrives in our life through an event that someone we know tells us about.
>
> Today a colleague told me the story of her five-year-old daughter, Isabella who had trapped her finger in the door at home. She told us her husband returned to the hinge of the door to collect the section of finger that had been separated, while a neighbour looked after Isabella. He put the separated piece of finger in a freezer bag and cool box and took her (and the finger) to hospital where it was sewn back on.
>
> Isabella's mother, my colleague, who was not present at the scene but had a close relationship to the event, recounted the story. I reacted to her telling it by making involuntary facial expressions and sounds, as though I was actually witnessing the event. It was all very real to me although it was only being retold. The same is true of watching a documentary play. The audience see events at one remove but become so embroiled in the story that it seems like they are a part of it.

The passages in **Blackout** had a unique power. I went on to develop a further version of the musical with the testimony woven into the script and given to the characters in the story. It continued to showcase my songs and is now my most performed musical! [3]

Although I was a Drama teacher by profession and now a head of department I still had limited experience of "proper theatre". I had only for example seen three Shakespeare productions, which I had really admired! [4]

I say this to re-enforce the fact that I was not an avid theatregoer and had limited experience of seeing professional theatre, which is without doubt the best way of gaining a toolbox of ideas/skills. My toolbox was worryingly empty.

Music Teachers I worked with in schools naturally took on the role of Musical Director from me forcing me to become purely the "director".

I had no training as a director but gradually acquired some skills.

My experience was of directing scenes written by friends, improvised by cast or scenes from musicals where I gained confidence purely from positive reactions I received.

---

[3] Blackout is available from *www.SchoolplayProductions.co.uk* as a download.

[4] A magical production of Midsummer Nights Dream in Regents Park Open Air Theatre (1979); Richard Eyre's 1980 The Royal Court Hamlet with Jonathan Pryce as *Hamlet* where he conjured the guttural, ghostly voice of his father most incredibly; The RSC Bogdanov 1986 version of *Romeo and Juliet* where Benvolio enters on a motorbike and Tybalt in a sports car.)

The Story Behind - Too Much Punch For Judy by Mark Wheeller

My directing "skills" (1975-1982):

* To stage simple scenes where characters talked to each other naturalistically

* To make all scenes seem as real as possible

* To maintain a general awareness on the part of the performers of the presence of an audience

* To make the production seem important to the cast thus gaining commitment

* To create a positive/happy atmosphere and encourage people to want to remain involved.

The last two bullet points arose from the fear I had of people dropping out. I was well aware that one person leaving might lead to others wanting to do so as well and then the whole thing might fall apart. In retrospect they should be first on the list… a survival technique.

These simple productions were easy for me to mount. They relied on my having bags of enthusiasm and an ability to forge positive relationships with my cast. I was avoiding having to do any "real work" most effectively. I started to think I needed to do more to gain creative satisfaction that, up until this point, my songs had been offering me. Mounting my own documentary play would offer me that opportunity and compel me to direct more creatively as I would not be dealing with naturalistic dialogue. I would have to bring long sections of narrative to life and also stage seemingly impossible scenes.

At this time, the exam board drama exams I was using changed the way teachers had to assess secondary school drama. This change forced me to develop my limited experience of performance work.

Throughout my time at Stantonbury the Drama CSE exams had no requirement on the candidates to perform. The CSE (Mode 3) was a fantastic course and allowed me to be successful without any formal stagecraft knowledge/theory. The wholly improvisation course schooled me (and my students) effectively in facilitating discussions, constructing stories and developing dramatic ideas collaboratively. Though I didn't know it at the time this would prove invaluable to my becoming a playmaker.

The Story Behind - Too Much Punch For Judy by Mark Wheeller

When I moved to Epping in 1982 I inherited a CSE course, which had a performance element. Through observing my own CSE groups' performances, I started to become aware of non-naturalistic presentations they used and admired students' creativity. I applied their ideas as templates for my work.

I remember one "spontaneous" improvisation exam (where students were given ten minutes to "prepare") where two candidates developed a scene about shoplifting. They had a lot of information that needed to be conveyed in a limited timeframe. Barrie Sapsford (who was to be in the *Too Much Punch* cast and designed this book) and Tony Holland created a technique I later christened **Two Touch** or **Précis Theatre**.

Two Touch or Précis Theatre:

* An effective way of showing a long story in a concise manner – "cutting out the rubbish".

* Reduce all lines to a maximum of one or two words.

This stood out from all the other naturalistic presentations and, subsequently, I encouraged students to use this technique and applied it in my own plays.

My background was the drama classroom and so my scripts, consequently, have a devised "classroom" feel.

With no family at that time, I threw myself into unbelievable hours of commitment to this "voluntary activity" and expected the same from EYT members. We worked hard, perhaps obsessively together and gave it our all. The quality of our presentations mattered to us above almost everything else.

In my next project (*Race to Be Seen* - 1983-84 which became *Graham – World's Fastest Blind Runner!*)[5] my songs were relegated to a subsidiary role and the script took centre stage in my first fully-fledged documentary play.
I selected a core group from *Blackout* who were prepared to work closely with me for more than a year to research, write and perform this documentary play with music. We chose a local blind athlete, Graham Salmon, as our subject.

The content raised the importance of the production for my cast. Graham and his wife Marie attended rehearsals. There cannot be anything more significant than the telling of a famous (he wasn't really but it seemed like he should be!) persons story directly to that person. It forced the cast raise their game.

---

[5] Scripts available from **www.zincpublishing.co.uk**. Full production dvd available from www.wheellerplays.co.uk or Wheellerplays@gmail.com

The Story Behind - Too Much Punch For Judy by Mark Wheeller

We researched Graham's story, interviewing family, friends, teachers and collecting newspaper articles about him. We collected masses of information, which we organised chronologically and, using only those words, created what became a very dense script. It was fortunate that I also came into contact with an early version of Physical Theatre, which helped enliven this mass of words.

I chanced upon a theatrical production of **Kes (Kestrel for a Knave)**, which had been one of my favourite films. Andy Graham's SNAP Theatre Company were performing it in London. Although I hadn't heard of them I discovered that they were based just down the road from Epping, in Hertfordshire. I almost walked out, as there were only two others in the audience! I feared it was probably not going to be very good. I stayed purely because I'd spent money on the ticket, so settled down to dispose of an hour of my life. I could not have been more impressed.

SNAP Theatre Company

* The four cast members played not only people, but also props and scenery

* There were so many magic moments and one that was absolutely spine tingling:

An early bodyprop we used in **Race to Be Seen** where I expected the cast to be the seats despite how uncomfortable it was for them!

Two performers created a pedal bin. A third, playing the young boy searching for his missing kestrel entered and pressed the foot pedal (human foot) on the pedal bin. The lid opened (a pair of human arms) and as I recognised the little mechanical bounce of the bin lid, I sniggered. This was followed by a silence as we, in the audience, realised what the young lad had seen. The contrast between this moment of humour (from how the scene was presented; not the scene itself) and the high drama of his realisation could not have been more pronounced. His older brother had brutally murdered the kestrel and disposed of it in the pedal-bin.

Like Roy's documentary plays, this presentation worked on different levels:

* The story, which had already won me over

* The clever presentation, which impressed, amused and added to the entertainment

It cost nothing.

We could do this... and we did!

The Story Behind - Too Much Punch For Judy by Mark Wheeller

Knowing we were about to start work on *Race* I decided we should apply a second limiting rule (the first being to use only the words of those we had interviewed).

* To tell Graham's story with no real props or scenery

We had a cast of thirteen so we had potential for imaginative body scenery/props. This self-imposed limitation forced us to be more creative in our presentation.

Achieving this in *Race* prepared the way for *Too Much Punch*.

> The greatest challenge in this production was the need to stage different races. A play about a world champion athlete could not be performed without staging what seemed at the outset to be "impossible" scenes.
>
> Directing this play would require more imagination than the simple naturalistic scenes I had undertaken previously.
>
> My way of approaching such scenes *(adopted from Tony Key in 4R)* relies on raising the confidence of the cast to the extent that they end up believing that any challenges I throw at them can be overcome. I pass the buck, understating the difficulties that confront us.
>
> My drive to perform the story communicates a confidence that enables my casts to generate a way of staging it. John Rowley[6] was one *Race* cast member who played a significant part in developing the final 400 metres scene.
>
> John had the idea of:
>
> Physically exercising and tiring himself out in front of us and alongside a scene his group performed about the determination of a potential Olympic athlete. Our reaction, as we watched this, was incredible. We found ourselves adopting John's breathing pattern and empathising closely with his physical exertion.
>
> *Page to Stage*
>
> In the versions of the scene Epping Youth Theatre staged, we were not brave, or perhaps experienced enough, to exploit this idea properly and I imagine John felt it was lost forever. However, I remembered it, knowing it was the key to that scene. It became an inspirational stepping-stone to provide the foundation to all the subsequent 400 metre race scenes I staged.[7] It conveyed the essence of the event rather than its physical shape. This rehearsal was, though I didn't realise at the time, also the first piece of the jigsaw puzzle to stage the "impossible" accident scene in *Punch* (see Appendix).

---

(6) John Rowley is one of the many performers to go on to make a professional career out of acting having performed for the famous Brith Gof Company and more recently, The National Theatre of Wales.
(7) An impressive version of this scene using this idea as the starting point can be seen in the OYT production of Graham – World's Fastest Blind Runner - DVD available from Wheellerplays@gmail.com

The Story Behind - Too Much Punch For Judy by Mark Wheeller

We spent about 18 months creating the script for Race, staging and rehearsing Graham's amazing story. To ensure this level of endeavour had a better payoff than a three night run in our school hall, I arranged to:

* Tour the play to venues in areas linked with different moments of Graham's life

* Showcase it at the *Edinburgh Festival Fringe*

Edinburgh was actually the suggestion of Graham's former PE teacher, Bill Aitken, who was at that time the head teacher at the Royal Blind School in Edinburgh. I jumped on the idea realising that it would achieve the same level of raising importance as Lewisham Concert Hall had for 4R. Generously, Bill offered us accommodation in his school and helped us to find a venue to perform the play.

Performing at the Fringe offered:

☑ An outstanding platform

☑ The opportunity to see more Theatre

We were all so keen to learn. The experience of developing *Race* was invaluable for *Too Much Punch*.

One production we saw that year was the premiere of John Godber's *Up and Under* (Hull Truck). I wanted to see how they staged a rugby match, which was, I felt, a similar challenge to our having to stage Graham's races.

Up and Under won a Fringe First and provided me with an education in stagecraft! Unbeknown to me at the time, John had also been a Drama teacher and had written both this and *Bouncers* before he left to become the director of Hull Truck. His plays were written imaginatively, with moments of non-naturalism and, like ours, for a company with a limited budget.

Hull Truck performances were in a different league to anything I had seen before. The audience were cheering by the end of the play, rooting for the team to win in a way we had never managed with Graham's final 400-metre race. [8] I was sitting in an auditorium watching a form of theatre, unlike West End Musicals whose budgets we could never match, that we could aspire to.

John Godber and Hull Truck opened my eyes to the potential of plays without songs. It became my obsession to reach this standard… and, like Hull Truck, to be awarded a Fringe First.

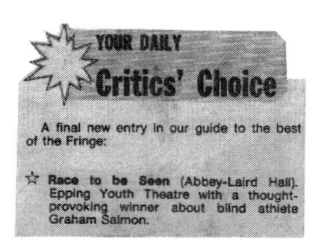

Evening News
THURSDAY, AUGUST 30, 1984

YOUR DAILY Critics' Choice

A final new entry in our guide to the best of the Fringe:

☆ **Race to be Seen** (Abbey-Laird Hall). Epping Youth Theatre with a thought-provoking winner about blind athlete Graham Salmon.

Race To Be Seen: Abbey-Laird

Out of sight out of mind sums up some attitudes to the disabled and this inspirational play from the Epping Youth Theatre smashes down these barriers.

The young cast put on a convincing performance that belies their years. Any danger of the piece being swamped in sentimentality vanishes with realistic touch in this documentary-style production.

They tell us the story of blind British athlete Graham Salmon who fought his handicap to end up holding world records for the blind at 100 and 400 metres.

Graham not only provided the theme for this moving theatrical event. He also co-wrote the beautifully sung songs which illuminate his story of true grit.

---

(8) In a later OYT production, Olympic athlete Roger Black attended and said he had found himself pumping his arms along with the race as he became involved in Graham's running.

The Story Behind - Too Much Punch For Judy by Mark Wheeller

The sponsorship that **Race** attracted enabled us to equip our small converted classroom with two lighting bars, a dimmer rack, lighting board and brand new lights. No longer would we need to perform our more intimate plays in an oversized and old-fashioned school hall. We painted the classroom black (without permission as I remember) and finally, just in time for **Too Much Punch**, it became a bona-fide Drama Studio, complete with fire doors!

Blackout and **Race** developed my practice significantly, despite the lack of physical levels in either! I sent Race off to be considered for publication, cheekily telling Longmans that there had been interest from other publishers when I hadn't sent it to anyone else! I said that it seemed appropriate for a local publisher (they were based in nearby Harlow) to take this community production on and invited them to see a performance. To my delight they attended and then published it. I thought I had made it (I hadn't. My first royalty cheque wasn't paid, as it didn't reach the £1 minimum!) and, flushed with this achievement, I was greedy for more success.

The songs in Race made it a hybrid play/musical and inhibited its success in published form. Only the lyrics were included in the text, so anyone performing it would be deterred from using them. Anyone wanting to stage a play would be put off because it had musical numbers in it. I decided my next EYT production should have no songs. **Too Much Punch** became that play and the first to be performed in our Drama Studio, with an audience capacity of 35!

On Sunday 29th September 1985 I held the first meeting for my new Epping Youth Theatre team. This group was convened from the most committed people from a musical we had presented the previous term. Musicals were now serving as a long-winded audition process for these, more challenging projects.

We arranged to meet at EYT member, Kim Baker's house. Mick, her father and a recovering alcoholic, had agreed to introduce us to the broad theme of the new play; alcohol – use and misuse. He openly expressed his doubts about how successful this might be, but offered his complete support.

People often ask me where I get "inspiration" for my plays. I don't think it is inspiration at all. It is much more being open to and seizing on ideas. **Too Much Punch** has a typical background:

* *In a drama class Kim created a scene re-constructing a moment in her family life revealing her dad to be an alcoholic*

* *Knowing I had been impressed she asked me if I'd be interested in EYT talking to her parents and then researching a play about alcoholism.*

The Story Behind - Too Much Punch For Judy by Mark Wheeller

Mick talked for 3 hours and gave us much food for thought. Some of his escapades were horrifying. He had traveled a long way to reflect on his experiences and relate them to us in the cold light of day. As I listened, I realised much was already there in embryonic form and would make engaging theatre. We were stunned into a silence that Mick misread as boredom.

This taught me a valuable lesson:

The signals we communicate to our subjects <u>MUST BE INTENTIONAL</u>

In the following weeks we:

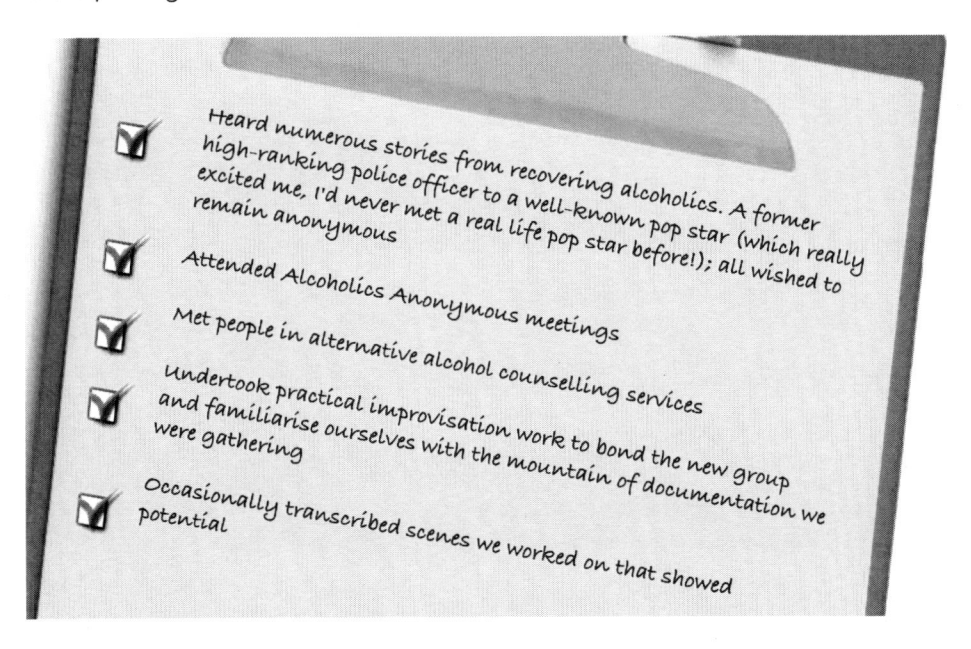

- ☑ Heard numerous stories from recovering alcoholics. A former high-ranking police officer to a well-known pop star (which really excited me, I'd never met a real life pop star before!); all wished to remain anonymous
- ☑ Attended Alcoholics Anonymous meetings
- ☑ Met people in alternative alcohol counselling services
- ☑ Undertook practical improvisation work to bond the new group and familiarise ourselves with the mountain of documentation we were gathering
- ☑ Occasionally transcribed scenes we worked on that showed potential

We were fumbling around in the dark, but heading towards a play that would explore alcohol abuse through the experiences of those who knew best. I was thorough, thorough enough to explore a new lead in early December, when we had completed our research.

Historical and Social

* Drink driving in 1985 did not have the profile it has today
* There was an annual Christmas television campaign but that was the only time drink driving was highlighted
* Although it wasn't socially acceptable, more people casually drove drunk or over the limit

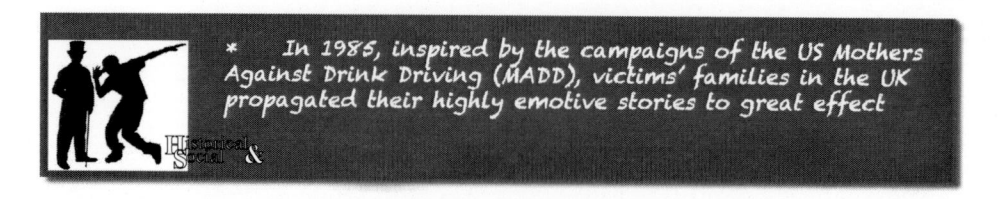

The Story Behind - Too Much Punch For Judy by Mark Wheeller

> *In 1985, inspired by the campaigns of the US Mothers Against Drink Driving (MADD), victims' families in the UK propagated their highly emotive stories to great effect*

I remember watching these early broadcasts on TV in December 1985 as the centrepiece of that year's Christmas drink drive campaign. I was annoyed with myself for having failed to realise this should be a part of our agenda. Families who had lost relatives expressed their emotions openly.

The stories were tragic and exposed a lack of justice.

"It was a head-on collision. In the ambulance, the driver said:

"I thought I was on a roundabout."

He was double the legal limit of alcohol... absolutely blotto!

He pleaded guilty, but only charged for excess alcohol. The fact that he killed someone did not even appear in the court hearing.

We have no other family. Just imagine how you'd feel if someone you loved very much was killed and died in dreadful circumstances like that and the person that did it was charged £125, you think, is that all she's worth?"

Audrey and Derek Probart (CADD)

I was determined to see if it we could find a local story. To that end I approached our schools Police Liaison Officer who put me onto PC Chris Caten. It was he who led me to Toni Poulton. Toni's was a case full of internal drama.
Tony was both victim and perpetrator.

Toni had killed her own sister. Both had been drinking on the night in question but Toni drove them both home.

Her intention was to protect Jo, who was already up for another drinking and driving charge. It was a highly emotive story.

Joanna (left) and Toni

The Story Behind - Too Much Punch For Judy by Mark Wheeller

It was a story Toni was willing to tell:

"Chris Caten explained that there was a local playwright looking for a story about drinking and driving. He wasn't sure I'd want to do it but he knew me quite well and thought it was worth sounding me out. I thought, well, I will, especially as Chris thought it was such a good idea. You've got to tell the truth haven't you? If you're wrong, admit it!
I didn't view the details of the accident as private. I'd dropped a bollock and it didn't matter to me how many people knew, as long as it would do some good somewhere along the line".

Toni Marriott (Poulton).

EYT in rehearsal for **Quenchers**

Mark Wheeller, Christmas 1985, working on the **Quenchers** *script*

The Story Behind - Too Much Punch For Judy by Mark Wheeller

2. Too Much Punch for Judy - The research

Some of the Epping Youth Theatre members I had recruited for this project had been in three or four previous EYT productions. Some had no production experience but had impressed me in school drama lessons.

> "The absence of any complete script at the beginning of rehearsals and the sheer necessity of providing a cracking show at the end remains a frightening situation, though each year we manage to get away with it!"
>
> Peter Cheeseman - Former Artistic Director of Victoria Theatre Stoke on Trent and Documentary Theatre guru!

* John Rowley, 19 when we started, was the oldest

* Jo Dumelow (who I called Jodi – Jo D) was the youngest, at only 12.

From re-reading my diary I have discovered I was concerned by the "power" I handed to the leaders. I feared them taking over, leaving no role for me. This set in motion a growing feeling that I had come to the end of the road in what I could achieve at Epping, which now, I find very odd. Having experienced people around me, with their own opinions, was obviously a learning curve for the 27-year-old Mark Wheeller. Was/am I that much of a control freak? Was I more comfortable working with less experienced people? If so, then that is very different from how I am now, where I could easily be accused of using those with experience as a crutch! To achieve what we did then was, I now realise, reliant on those with more experience. I needed them there to challenge me!

Whatever my misgivings were, I remained outwardly confident to everyone… I think. I was certainly encouraged by the interest we were garnering from the authorities, even in those early days.

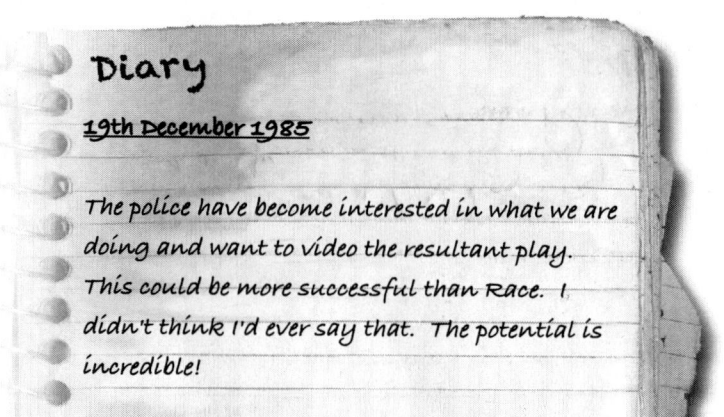

> **Diary**
>
> **19th December 1985**
>
> The police have become interested in what we are doing and want to video the resultant play. This could be more successful than Race. I didn't think I'd ever say that. The potential is incredible!

The police interest was aroused when I sounded them out about using some drink drive stories. The drink-drive campaign needed as much publicity as possible and they spotted an opportunity. The meeting between Toni and I happened in the Christmas holidays.

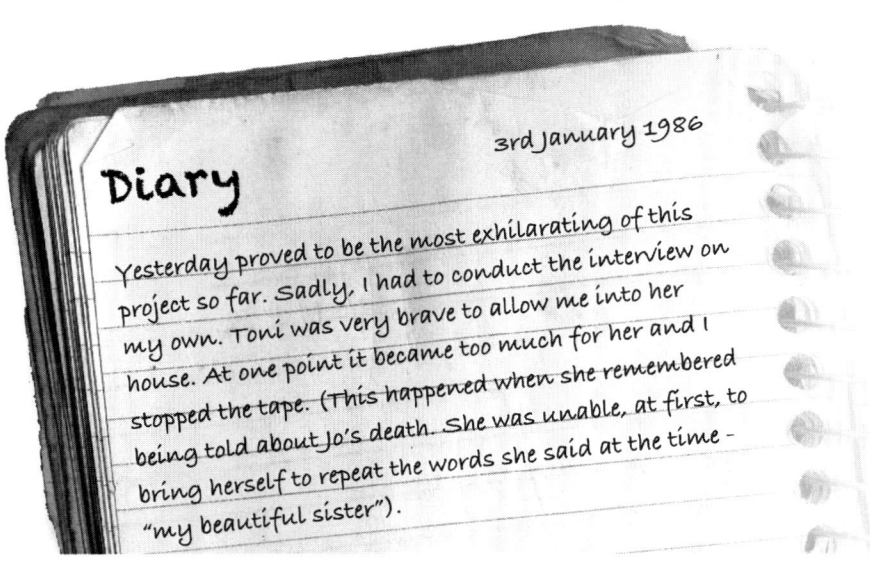

The Story Behind - Too Much Punch For Judy by Mark Wheeller

> **Diary** 3rd January 1986
>
> Yesterday proved to be the most exhilarating of this project so far. Sadly, I had to conduct the interview on my own. Toni was very brave to allow me into her house. At one point it became too much for her and I stopped the tape. (This happened when she remembered being told about Jo's death. She was unable, at first, to bring herself to repeat the words she said at the time – "my beautiful sister").

I always ensure that in any production of the play the person playing Judy knows this and breaks down on saying these words.

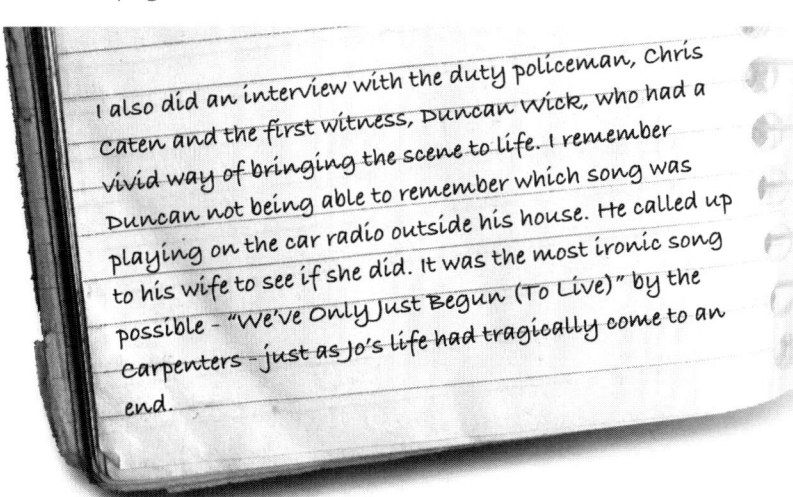

> I also did an interview with the duty policeman, Chris Caten and the first witness, Duncan Wick, who had a vivid way of bringing the scene to life. I remember Duncan not being able to remember which song was playing on the car radio outside his house. He called up to his wife to see if she did. It was the most ironic song possible – "We've Only Just Begun (To Live)" by the Carpenters – just as Jo's life had tragically come to an end.

It must have been difficult for Toni, as she had never talked to anyone outside her family about this accident. I felt having an entourage of Youth Theatre members gawping at her as she spoke would be inappropriate, which is why I conducted her interview alone. Working alone in the interviews contradicted my philosophy of cast involvement in every aspect of the production and accidentally led me to hold the reigns for this part of the project. I retained a strong editorial control over the writing of this section of the play.

The Story Behind - Too Much Punch For Judy by Mark Wheeller

Not only was I the only one to have a unique knowledge of the material but I had also the experience of developing a successful documentary play (**Race**) by this time.

I took every opportunity to encourage Toni to remember dialogue, or at least approximate it.

I had a clear vision of how this scene needed to be written, which led to a permanent change in my practice.

* The collaborative element in my Youth Theatre work would, from this point on, become about the staging of scenes, rather than the writing of them

Chris arranged an interview the following day with PC Abrahams, the young policeman who was with him that fateful evening and the Sister who had been on duty at the hospital that night. North Weald is a small village so, unsurprisingly, they all knew Toni and Jo and had vivid memories of the event, even though over two years had passed.

I conducted these additional interviews alone to organise them more quickly. The last thing I wanted was more delays to demotivate my cast who were understandably impatient to get on and had already spent a whole term interviewing and transcribing material and doing little practical work. Some had dropped out, possibly because of this "slow progress". I was fearful more might leave which might threaten the whole project.

On January 5th my diary records that John Rowley and I spent an evening working out a draft chronology of the play, which we presented to the cast the following week. The accident scene was placed at the end of the play and that never changed. I remember feeling the rest of the play would not reach the same high standard as this section.

Had I been working alone I would have dropped everything but Toni's story. However, with all the effort everyone had put into developing the other material I did not feel able to do that.

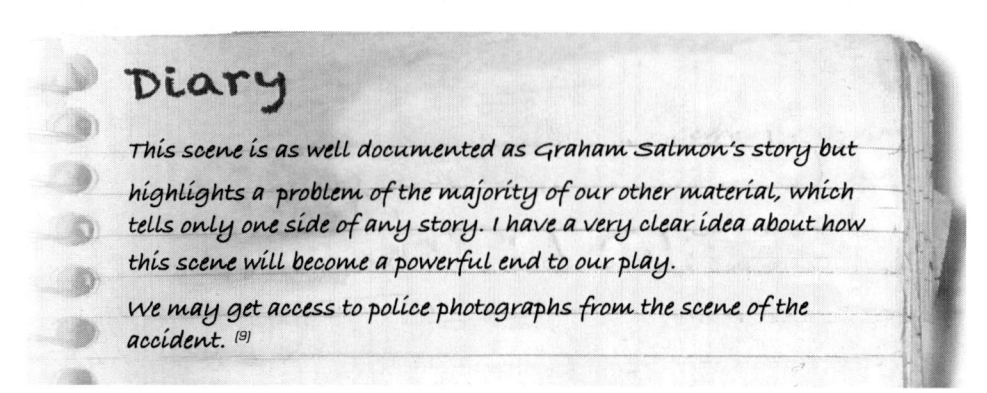

Diary

This scene is as well documented as Graham Salmon's story but highlights a problem of the majority of our other material, which tells only one side of any story. I have a very clear idea about how this scene will become a powerful end to our play.

We may get access to police photographs from the scene of the accident. [9]

---

(9) Pages 165-167 (with permission of the police)

The Story Behind - Too Much Punch For Judy by Mark Wheeller

I was really keen to get these images. It is a curious concept to place authentic pictures within a re-enactment. It is one that you might think, on first consideration, would be in danger of deflecting focus from the action on stage and moreover one that might highlight all that is not real in it.

I believed there were many advantages to using authentic images projected onto a screen behind the performers from my experience of seeing the technique first hand in Roy's documentary plays.

> The use of authentic images brought a reality to the re-enactment and served to engage me more fully with the theatrical presentation.
>
> Involuntarily I superimposed the images onto what I saw on stage making the theatrical event seem more real, more emotive and more affecting
>
> The use of these images was integral to the success of the documentary plays Roy presented because they were actually from/of the event itself

As a direct result of witnessing Roy's use of authentic images in his documentary plays I added them to all my post-Stantonbury productions.

> I added authentic images of the evacuation and wartime posters to the Epping Youth Theatre production of *Blackout* This confirmed my belief that the stage picture becomes richer, even though these images were not specifically of the story of Rachel, our fictional evacuee.
>
> A photographer took sepia photos of Youth Theatre members playing the roles in Blackout in Epping Forest. These pictures were used in the production as though they were of the real evacuees. Although they added to the production I was aware they lacked authenticity because they were mock-ups.
>
> The real Graham Salmon was projected onto a screen at the back of the stage of Race to be Seenwhile the performer presented the role of Graham on stage. The audience would, I hoped, merge the "real" photographic image onto our performer, making him more "real" and believable on stage

I felt that the powerful police images of Toni's accident (which left nothing to the imagination) would act like scenery adding further detail to the stage picture, making the scene more "real".

It was only later that I became aware of Brecht's *Epic Theatre* and *"Verfremdungseffekt"*, or as Martin Esslin describes it in his book *A Choice of Evils* the *Distantiation Effect*, which I prefer to the more popular *"alienation effect"* but has off-putting emotional overtones.

The Story Behind - Too Much Punch For Judy by Mark Wheeller

Brecht's Verfremdungseffekt:
"*Epic Theatre is strictly historical; it constantly reminds the audience that it is merely getting a report of past events. (The audience is encouraged to maintain) a separate existence by being kept apart, alien, strange, - therefore the producer must strive to produce by all the means at his disposal effects which will keep the audience separated from the action. By abandoning the pretense that the audience is eavesdropping on actual events, by openly admitting that the theatre is a theatre and not a world itself, the Brechtian stage approximates to the lecture hall which the audiences will enter in the expectation that they will be informed.*" (10)

I am glad I came across this theory after witnessing the practice, as I am not sure I would have warmed to it. My thoughts (for what they are worth) on the use of images in relation to the Verfremdungseffekt are (currently) as follows:

* Using original photographs in a production reminds the audience that the stage action is not real but a re-enactment of real events

* Although the use of these images disengages the audience from the theatrical action (by reminding them the actors are not real) the audiences relationship with the content of the play becomes more intense

* I would not want to disengage my audience from emotional involvement in the production. An audience member being moved to laughter or tears is one of the clearest indicators of success for performers or myself as the writer/director I want my audiences to be engrossed, moved and wrapped up in the situation to the exclusion of anything else. This will not happen at every moment, but there are some moments where it is essential. I want them, at times, to forget they are in a theatre and to be transported into the world of the play. Documentary plays include a range of approaches and have moments of naturalism where this can occur

* (I'm jumping ahead but in *Too Much Punch For Judy* an example of this is the scene where Chris Caten reveals to Toni/Judy that her sister has been killed in the accident. This scene is entirely naturalistic, in contrast to the narrative passages)

* I want the impact of the production to remain long after it is completed. I want my audience to reflect on it and be moved to action after it is finished.

---

(10) From Martin Esslin's seminal book *A Choice of Evils*. The chapter *The Brechtian Theatre – It's Theory and Practice* makes outstanding further reading.

The Story Behind - Too Much Punch For Judy by Mark Wheeller

Re-reading the chapter in Martin Esslin's book today, I am reminded what a debt Documentary Theatre has to Brecht and his theories.

I was feeling "positive" as we moved into the second phase of our work; editing the testimony into a play. Even at this early stage Longmans (the publishers who had taken on *Race to be Seen*) said they wanted to see the script once it was completed. Even with little experience I felt I was gaining the interest of the "big boys". It made me feel supremely confident. Paul Elliott, a 17-year-old EYT cast member wrote his A-level extended essay on documentary theatre, quoted me at the time.

This quote applies equally well to me as a writer as to the school students I refer to:

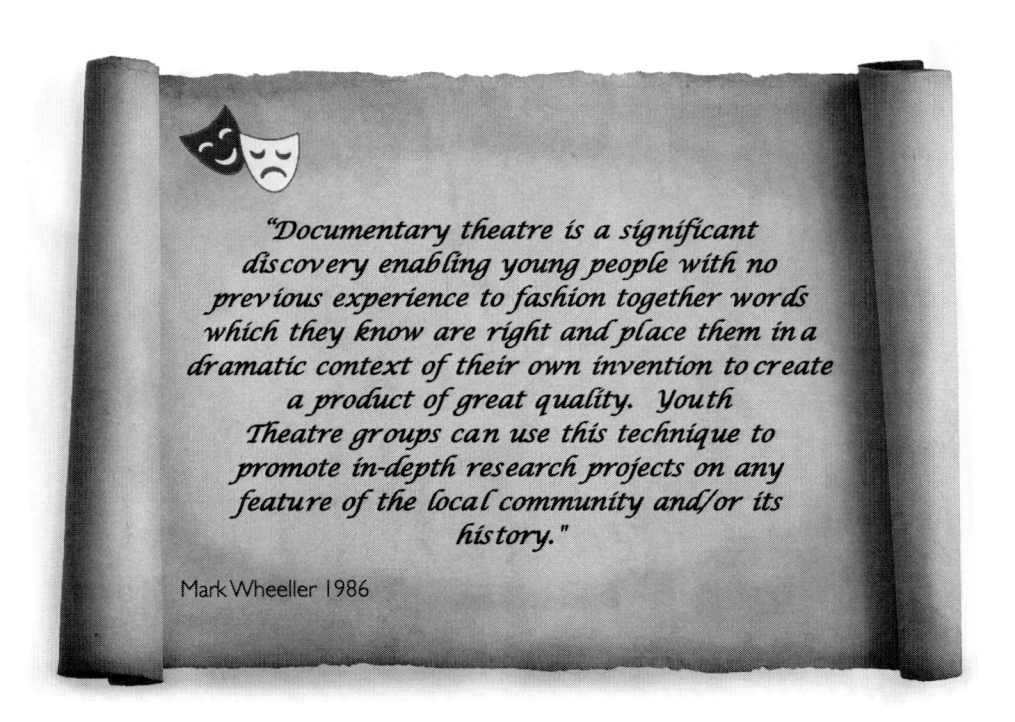

"Documentary theatre is a significant discovery enabling young people with no previous experience to fashion together words which they know are right and place them in a dramatic context of their own invention to create a product of great quality. Youth Theatre groups can use this technique to promote in-depth research projects on any feature of the local community and/or its history."

Mark Wheeller 1986

The Story Behind - Too Much Punch For Judy by Mark Wheeller

3. Quenchers - Preparation

Inter-relationships and atmosphere are central to any successful project. A strong leader must also inspire confidence and, to experiment successfully, must be prepared to risk failure if genuine progress is to be made.

After a full term of collecting materials and doing limited practical work based on them, some of EYT were putting forward ideas but there were also those who merely went along with them.

> "Create a pleasant working environment; surround yourself with people who will encourage you; persevere; demand respect; don't be afraid, realise it is a learning process, nothing will ever be perfect."
>
> (Kate Bush advice to young songwriters – Classic Rock Magazine)

I was aware this had to be addressed to encourage all to become more active participants in the development of the project.
I focussed our first meeting of 1986, not on the content of the play itself but on encouraging people, particularly the younger, less experienced cast members, to offer more of a contribution.

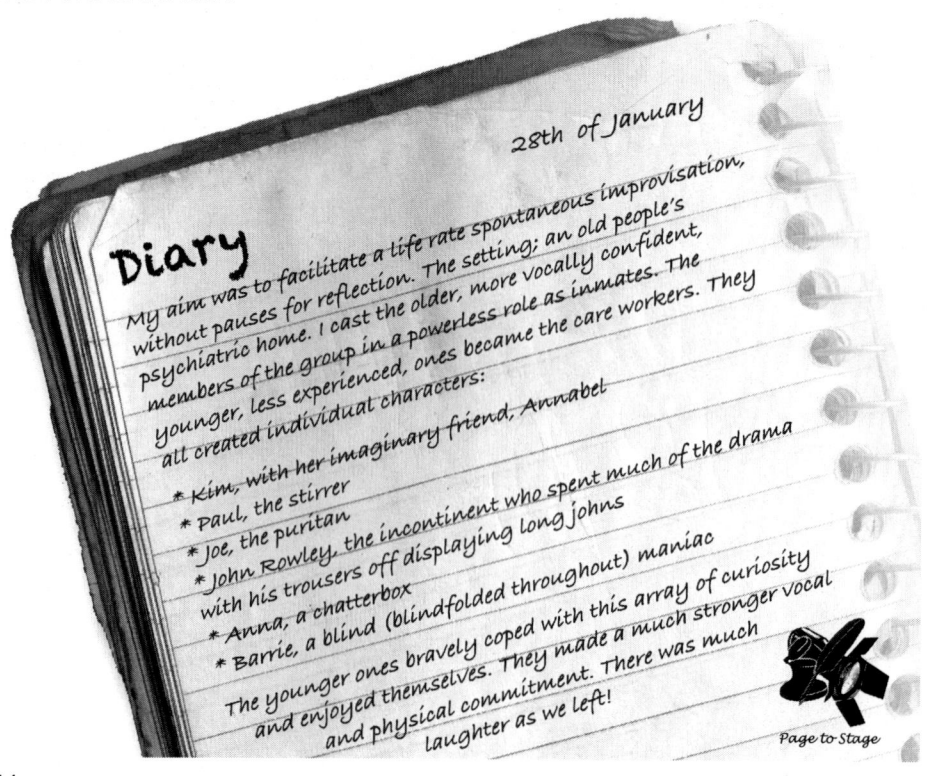

Diary — 28th of January

My aim was to facilitate a life rate spontaneous improvisation, without pauses for reflection. The setting; an old people's psychiatric home. I cast the older, more vocally confident, members of the group in a powerless role as inmates. The younger, less experienced, ones became the care workers. They all created individual characters:

* Kim, with her imaginary friend, Annabel
* Paul, the stirrer
* Joe, the puritan
* John Rowley, the incontinent who spent much of the drama with his trousers off displaying long johns
* Anna, a chatterbox
* Barrie, a blind (blindfolded throughout) maniac

The younger ones bravely coped with this array of curiosity and enjoyed themselves. They made a much stronger vocal and physical commitment. There was much laughter as we left!

The Story Behind - Too Much Punch For Judy by Mark Wheeller

This session worked well, forcing the less experienced to be more confident alongside their elders. All cast members, began to make a more equal contribution to the development sessions.

A few weeks later I conducted a *Stanislavski* session on emotional memory. This was strange for me as the production was always to be more *Brechtian*, but I wanted the performers to relate to the strong emotions the characters were experiencing. Frustratingly I didn't record in detail what we did but I am fairly sure it involved:

* Walking along an imaginary line representing each person's (real) life story

* Along their individual lifeline marking key moments

* The participant returns to the place representing the strongest emotional experience remaining there, alone privately to re-live the moment in as much detail as possible.

That emotional experience was then applied to open-ended improvisations that I recorded in my diary:

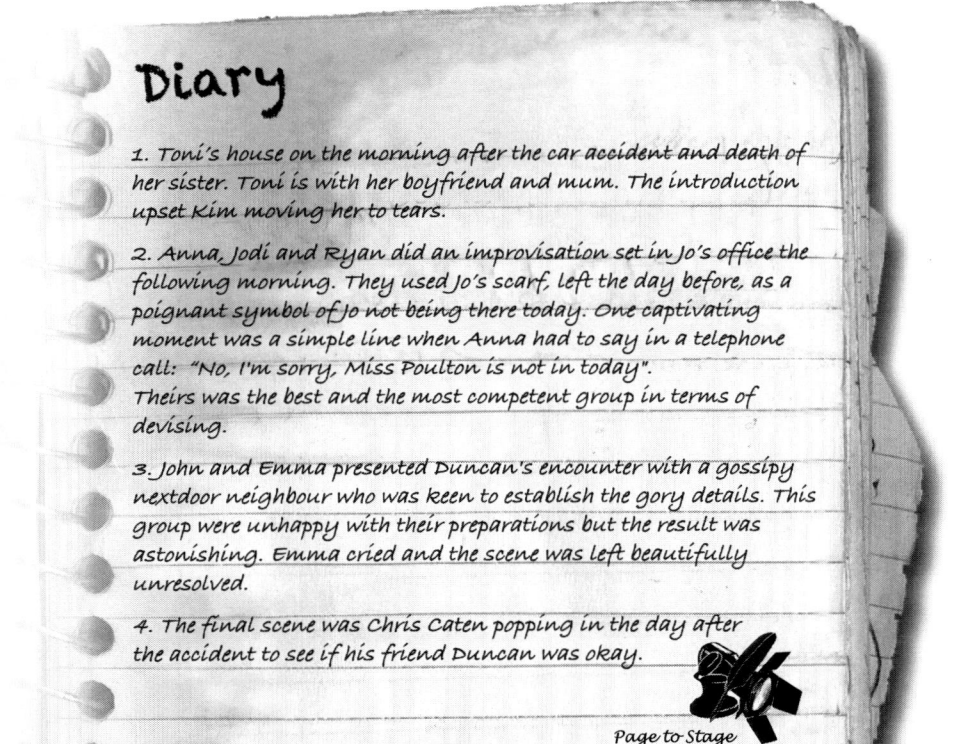

Diary

1. Toni's house on the morning after the car accident and death of her sister. Toni is with her boyfriend and mum. The introduction upset Kim moving her to tears.

2. Anna, Jodi and Ryan did an improvisation set in Jo's office the following morning. They used Jo's scarf, left the day before, as a poignant symbol of Jo not being there today. One captivating moment was a simple line when Anna had to say in a telephone call: "No, I'm sorry, Miss Poulton is not in today".
Theirs was the best and the most competent group in terms of devising.

3. John and Emma presented Duncan's encounter with a gossipy nextdoor neighbour who was keen to establish the gory details. This group were unhappy with their preparations but the result was astonishing. Emma cried and the scene was left beautifully unresolved.

4. The final scene was Chris Caten popping in the day after the accident to see if his friend Duncan was okay.

The Story Behind - Too Much Punch For Judy by Mark Wheeller

I felt we were ready to begin work on developing the play. I decided to start by creating the final section of the play first. Usual practice, for me, would be to work chronologically. I imagine I started here to help my/our confidence or perhaps I was scared of attempting anything else!

* I asked everyone to say what part they would like and discussed where two or more expressed interest

* Parts were agreed and allocated, a process I still use to give the cast responsibility from the outset. People opt into what they feel they can best manage. Kim took on the role of Toni. She was perfect with her natural confidence and a rough edge that was in step with Toni. It was also "right", as without Kim and her family, who were now proactively generating sponsorship for us, this project would never have started

* Cast members took the interview transcript for their character and cut and pasted it literally, (this was before computers) into the chronological order. This task was completed in two, three-hour sessions

* Everyone became an expert on his or her character

* Collating unaltered segments from the interviews, we developed a chronological patchwork for me to return home and further develop

Page to Stage

On the 12th February I took a copy of my draft "script" to Toni:

> Toni read silently. She was choked at times and approved of how we were moving forward:
>
> "Some of the lines you've given people are just how they'd say them."
>
> That is the strength of the documentary method! She made no alterations.
>
> She was concerned by Duncan's "bloody woman... she was that drunk!" speech and what impression that may convey of her! I found this surprising given the context, but offered her the opportunity to make a retrospective comment if she wanted to but she declined.
>
> Kim, who came with me, was not outward in expressing her enthusiasm for what we are doing. I cannot tell what she is thinking. Shyness?
>
> This afternoon Chris Caten read the script and worked with me to develop his dialogue.
>
> He said he wants us to be emotional in our performances as that is how it was. He thought Race to be Seen was "described" rather than "felt".
>
> I spent the evening upgrading the scene and making it as "right" as possible given the extra input.

The Story Behind - Too Much Punch For Judy by Mark Wheeller

I also referred to titles we were considering:

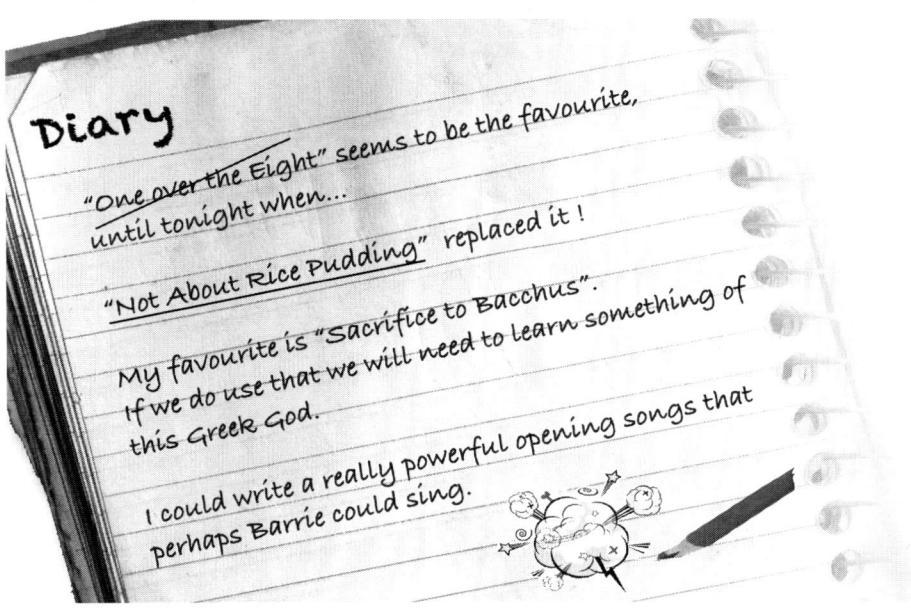

> **Diary**
>
> "One over the Eight" seems to be the favourite, until tonight when...
>
> "Not About Rice Pudding" replaced it!
>
> My favourite is "Sacrifice to Bacchus". If we do use that we will need to learn something of this Greek God.
>
> I could write a really powerful opening songs that perhaps Barrie could sing.

I was still trying to get a song in there… somewhere!!!

There were also surprising signs of disillusion from Kim who started to miss the odd rehearsal. Surely she would not mess up this opportunity. We discovered that she had a new boyfriend and I wondered if he was now taking priority. I wasn't too worried about it. Her parents were so involved and supportive and… well… she was playing Toni! How could she mess up that opportunity?

Once the drink drive section (amounting to about 15 minutes stage time[11]) was completed, we moved forward with the first and main, part of the play. The development of this was genuinely a collaborative effort. I had little input other than being an outside eye and helping with the overarching structure to ensure there was variation and contrast; comedy/serious etc.

I genuinely hadn't got a clue how (or if) it would turn out, but hid any insecurity I might have had from the cast (as I always do) with a steely determination. I was totally reliant on the devising skills of the group who continued to approach each scene with much imagination.

---

(11) The Too Much Punch for Judy section in Quenchers started with Jo and Judy leaving the aerobics class up to the scene where Judy returns home with her mum. Duncan's monologue about the roadies provided the ending. It had less detail than the final version of this section and no flashbacks.

The Story Behind - Too Much Punch For Judy by Mark Wheeler

The cast considered a range of different styles to maintain audience interest.

(Sadly neither were used in the final performance)

A cartoon style improvisation around a Health Education pack setting out the history of alcohol.

* Edited accounts of some of the recovering alcoholics we'd met.

On the 9th March two significant events occurred. I was suddenly placed in a situation where I was asked to help a cast member who was suffering from anorexia. I could find no information regarding organisations that may be able to help. There were no phone numbers listed under Anorexia in the phone directory. From what I was told, the girl's Doctor was equally in the dark, which I found shocking. This led to my commitment to develop what finally became *Hard to Swallow*; a script, which if published, would have a page saying whom to contact in the event of needing support… but that's another story.[12]

---

[12] *From what I have heard this girl has made a full recovery, but that certainly didn't happen in the course of this project, which was to go on for another 16 months. Hard to Swallow – Easy To Digest (2017), also published by Pping, tells the story of the development process behind Hard to Swallow.*

The Story Behind - Too Much Punch For Judy by Mark Wheeller

That same day I also came across an old Northern Ireland drink drive campaign poster shown below. (13)

I thought *Too Much Punch For Judy* was the perfect title for our play so showed the poster to the cast.

None liked it.

They said it was right for the drink drive section but not for the play as a whole.

I thought it was a golden opportunity for publicity purposes with the fictional childhood characters names implying a dark, intriguing content. I suggested that, as a compromise, we should entitle the final scene T*oo Much Punch For Judy*.

Although this was agreed, I knew no one in our audience would be aware of this.

---

(13) A woman who auditioned for the professional show, some years later, introduced herself to Ape Theatre Company as the model from this image. She finally saw the play when it was performed at the Gatehouse Pub in London by the JR Theatre Company and as I was there too… we met. I wished I'd taken a photo!

The Story Behind - Too Much Punch For Judy by Mark Wheeller

Although we had a draft of the script written by this point, we had not staged any of it. I had no idea how it would look or even if it would work with all the disparate sections linked together. I wasn't certain that we had anything worthwhile to take to Edinburgh.

Artistic concerns paled into significance as the financial ones confronted me.

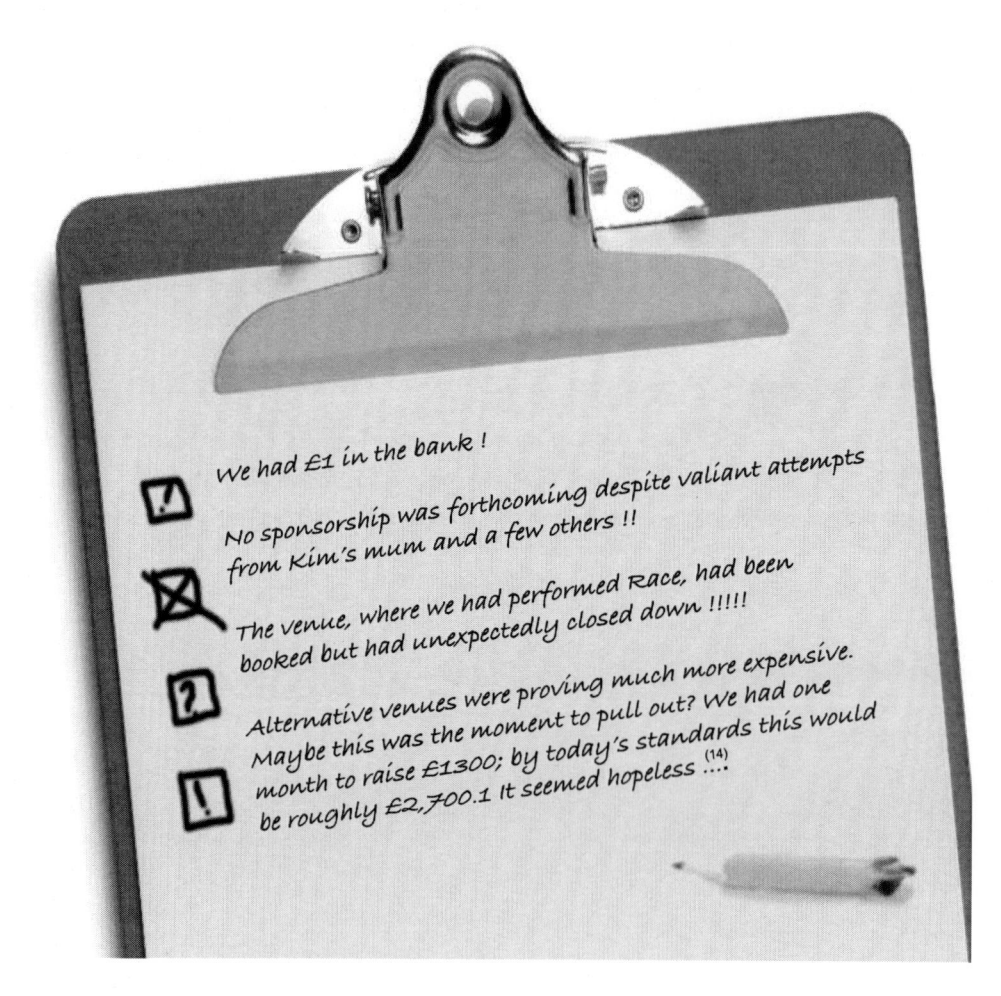

We had £1 in the bank !

No sponsorship was forthcoming despite valiant attempts from Kim's mum and a few others !!

The venue, where we had performed Race, had been booked but had unexpectedly closed down !!!!!

Alternative venues were proving much more expensive. Maybe this was the moment to pull out? We had one month to raise £1300; by today's standards this would be roughly £2,700.1 It seemed hopeless ....[14]

---

(14) Source: http://www.nationalarchives.gov.uk/currency/results1.asp#mid

The Story Behind - Too Much Punch For Judy by Mark Wheeller

We postponed work on the (still untitled) play, due to be performed in only three months time and focused our efforts on fundraising. The cast were more determined than I was to take it to Edinburgh; in those days I had hair, perhaps it was then that I pulled most of it out!

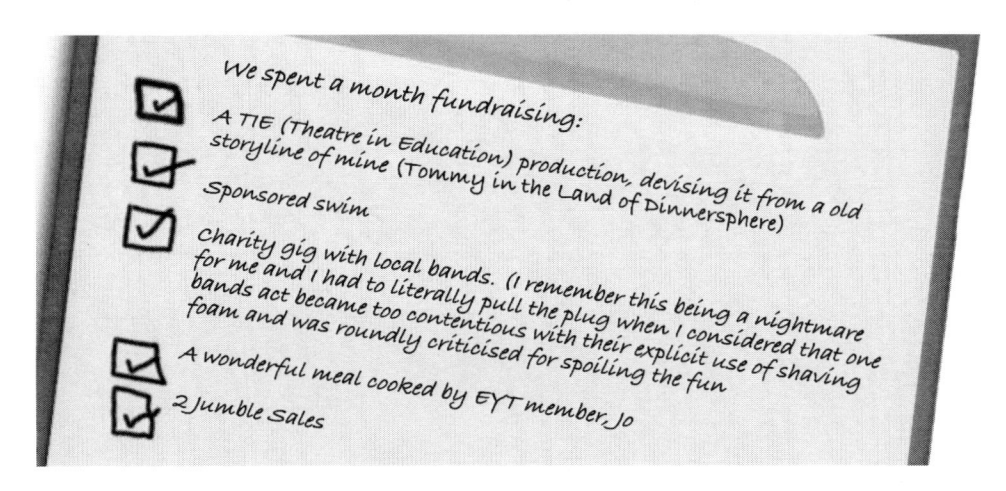

> We spent a month fundraising:
> - ☑ A TIE (Theatre in Education) production, devising it from a old storyline of mine (Tommy in the Land of Dinnersphere)
> - ☑ Sponsored swim
> - ☑ Charity gig with local bands. (I remember this being a nightmare for me and I had to literally pull the plug when I considered that one bands act became too contentious with their explicit use of shaving foam and was roundly criticised for spoiling the fun
> - ☑ A wonderful meal cooked by EYT member, Jo
> - ☑ 2 Jumble Sales

By the end of April we had raised nearly £1,500. It was such a determined effort that led me to record the following in my diary:

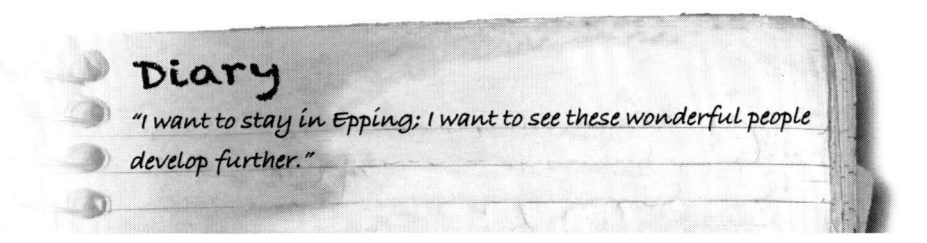

> **Diary**
> "I want to stay in Epping; I want to see these wonderful people develop further."

The cast gained invaluable performance experience presenting the TIE show and raised an impressive sum of money from ticket sales.

By the end of March the first draft of our script was printed out and ready for rehearsals and we had a title for it:

Quenchers.

I hastily sent it off to Longmans… too hastily, as it would undergo many significant improvements throughout the whole rehearsal period (and beyond). The version they saw was unrecognisable from any we performed.[16]

---

(15) *This later became Jamie in the Land of Dinnersphere now published by zincpublishing.co.uk.*
(16) *Any young people who have worked with me will testify my constant desire for perfection, changing scripts sometimes only moments before they go on stage.*

The Story Behind - Too Much Punch For Judy by Mark Wheeller

On the 27th April *Quenchers* was cast and we had our first read through, with only two and a half months before our first performance!

> **Diary**
>
> With the exception of Kim (Toni), the standard of reading was very low. The script seemed cold, empty and in places boring! Everyone thinks the history of alcohol scene is too long. John Rowley is pressing strongly to cut the pop star speech completely. I am resisting this with equal vigour. It is a strong introduction. Morally I feel obliged to keep it in and make it work as if it is cut that performer has little else to do.

Although we were running out of time the cast remained incredibly optimistic. Our venue in Week One of the Edinburgh Fringe had, by this time, been booked and although more expensive was central which should attract bigger audiences. We booked a second venue for Week 2, which was less central (and less expensive) but we were confident that by then we would have a reputation, so it would not matter as much. Oh the confidence!!!

On the 4th May we had our first rehearsal of the car crash:

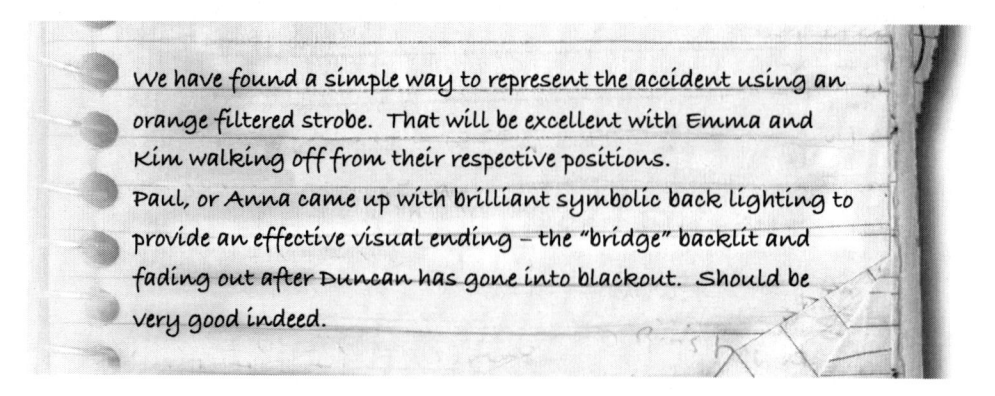

> We have found a simple way to represent the accident using an orange filtered strobe. That will be excellent with Emma and Kim walking off from their respective positions.
> Paul, or Anna came up with brilliant symbolic back lighting to provide an effective visual ending – the "bridge" backlit and fading out after Duncan has gone into blackout. Should be very good indeed.

I know this is not clear but what is interesting to note is that we were relying on lighting effects rather than any form of physical theatre. I imagine it was basically a glorified still image!

The Story Behind - Too Much Punch For Judy by Mark Wheeller

On the 7th May there was a further development from the *Institute of Alcohol Studies (IAS)* to whom I'd sent a copy of the script for comments.

> **Diary**
>
> The IAS feel the balance of the play is too negative. There is no alternative for non-drinkers. They have offered to develop a non-alcoholic cocktail drink called *Quenchers* to help redress this balance. We met tonight to develop a new 100% non-alcoholic *Quenchers* drink and scene. Great fun! Paul Elliott although ill tonight, worked hard and invented Captain Assertive and his sidekick.

Captain Assertive was our Superhero who battled against the Hooded Host and the parties he held offering no alternative to alcoholic drinks. Captain Assertive had an "assertive ray" offering instant assertiveness to refuse such drinks. The *Grange Hill* (remember Zammo?) *"Just Say No"* campaign of that era inspired this offering. Paul and Ryan had an opportunity to show off their comic genius!

Picture of Paul Elliott as Captain Assertive and Ryan Gilbey as his then unnamed sidekick.

The Story Behind - Too Much Punch For Judy by Mark Wheeller

Over the next few days I came across a very short story called, *The Bear Who Could Take It Or Leave It Alone* by James Thurber. This was the tale of an alcoholic bear that sobers up and becomes a temperance speaker. He goes so far in his views that he scares his own family with his dogma. This would provide a much-needed upbeat scene and placed just before *Too Much Punch For Judy* an effective contrast. I applied for copyright clearance, as I was concerned that we could never create something as good in the remaining two months.

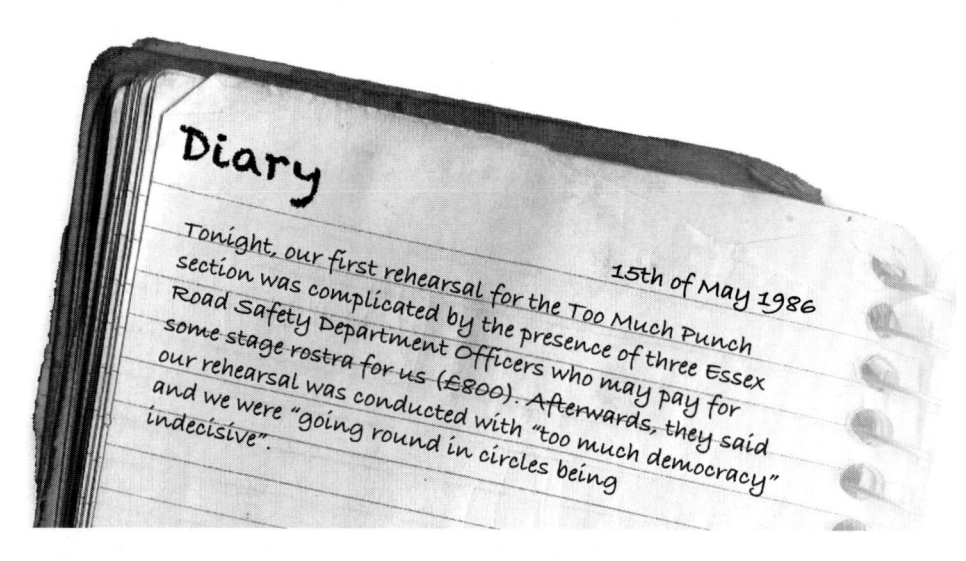

> **Diary**
>
> 15th of May 1986
>
> Tonight, our first rehearsal for the Too Much Punch section was complicated by the presence of three Essex Road Safety Department Officers who may pay for some stage rostra for us (£800). Afterwards, they said our rehearsal was conducted with "too much democracy" and we were "going round in circles being indecisive".

I remember it well.

It was frustrating that we couldn't show them any "product". (We had none to show!) These observers saw us struggling to figure out what to do. I thought we'd blown it.

Imagine my surprise when a few weeks later they contacted me saying they wanted to offer us £1000… enough to pay for the folding rostra and more!

The Story Behind - Too Much Punch For Judy by Mark Wheeller

Too Much Punch must have obviously been playing on my mind as we started to rehearse it.

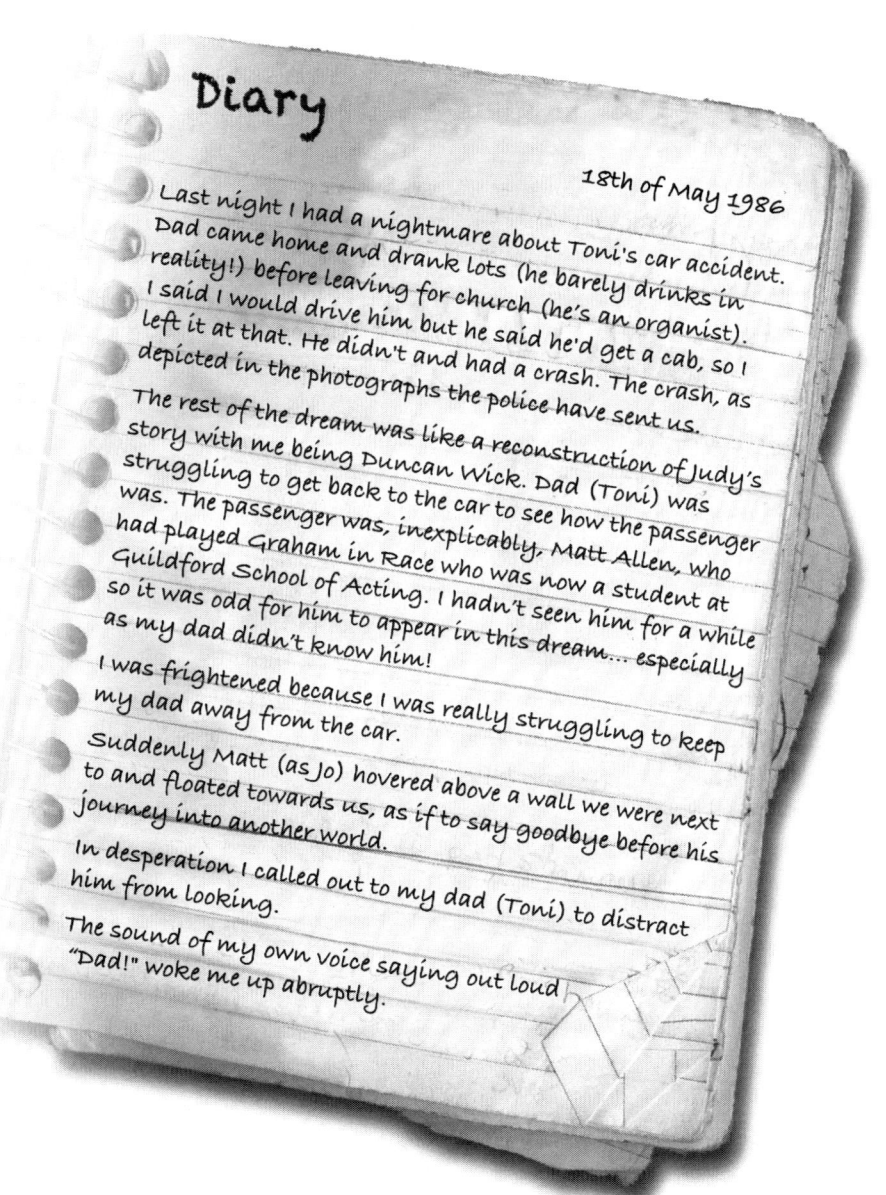

> **Diary**
>
> 18th of May 1986
>
> Last night I had a nightmare about Toni's car accident. Dad came home and drank lots (he barely drinks in reality!) before leaving for church (he's an organist). I said I would drive him but he said he'd get a cab, so I left it at that. He didn't and had a crash. The crash, as depicted in the photographs the police have sent us.
>
> The rest of the dream was like a reconstruction of Judy's story with me being Duncan Wick. Dad (Toni) was struggling to get back to the car to see how the passenger was. The passenger was, inexplicably, Matt Allen, who had played Graham in Race who was now a student at Guildford School of Acting. I hadn't seen him for a while so it was odd for him to appear in this dream... especially as my dad didn't know him!
>
> I was frightened because I was really struggling to keep my dad away from the car.
>
> Suddenly Matt (as Jo) hovered above a wall we were next to and floated towards us, as if to say goodbye before his journey into another world.
>
> In desperation I called out to my dad (Toni) to distract him from looking.
>
> The sound of my own voice saying out loud "Dad!" woke me up abruptly.

This nightmare played on my mind but served to inspire a key directorial moment in the scene between Duncan and Toni just after the accident.

The Story Behind - Too Much Punch For Judy by Mark Wheeller

The lasting impression was that I was not strong enough to hold onto my Dad (Toni). I was aware that if I was unable to hold onto him he would get to see the corpse in the car. It petrified me! Suddenly I saw this scene from Duncan's point of view.

When we came to block the scene roughly, I secretly said to Kim (Toni) that she must struggle so hard that, in the next run through, she must escape from John (Duncan). She did and of course it ruined the scene.

I told them about my dream and said to John (Duncan) that he must at all costs hold on to her no matter how much she struggles with him. She must be really trying to get away to give the scene an added power with the sense that something might actually go wrong, which of course it could. Leaving that to chance gave the scene an incredible tension.

Once Toni (Kim) calmed down I suggested she should stop struggling as she was worn out. The exertion he put into holding onto her had an unexpected side effect. It had a physiological effect on the way he delivered the monologue starting:

"I thought she was going to get so hysterical that I just wouldn't be able to cope... but she didn't actually; she just seemed to go limpish and cry."

He was out of breath and his voice became shaky. It made the monologue much more powerful. Finally, I asked Kim to underscore his speech with audible sobbing. It generated an incredibly tense moment in the play; inspired by a nightmare.

I have since applied this concept to scenes where a similarly powerful speech is to be delivered but is not preceded by vigorous action. Simply the performer needs to take a very deep breath and exhaling nearly all of the breath before delivering on the last part of the breath. It will give a similar effect.

If you're reading this alone with no one looking, try this technique with the line from the script above. In fact even if people are with you, try it and see how they react to your sudden outburst of a dramatic line!

John and I worked on Duncan's monologues a lot. They lend themselves to a gentle, underplayed "demonstration" performance manner (A la Brecht) with plenty of opportunities for contrasts within the speech. One means of exploring these was to ask John to revel in telling the story. In my experience people often enjoy telling gory stories. This offered him new options and to "lift" the words off the page.

Page to Stage

The Story Behind - Too Much Punch For Judy by Mark Wheeller

Delivering Monologues

> So many characters in the play have to deliver monologues that I decided to run a session on telling our stories. We used stories that were personal to us and went on to try to capture some of their essence in speeches within the script. The stories we told were <u>very</u> personal. The cast member who was going through anorexia talked about that and John and I told our respective sides of an argument we had in Edinburgh.
>
> Paul went away with the idea of "respect for the stories" and the responsibility that entails. I left with a vivid impression of the nervousness of telling the stories plus the courage of being so honest. I hope this can lead to a more subtle portrayal than merely "telling" the audience.

Page to Stage

Following the success of the media coverage for *Race*, I was proactive in contacting local and national news programs. Eventually I had a bite, but on the same evening, a new concern about Kim's commitment reared its head.

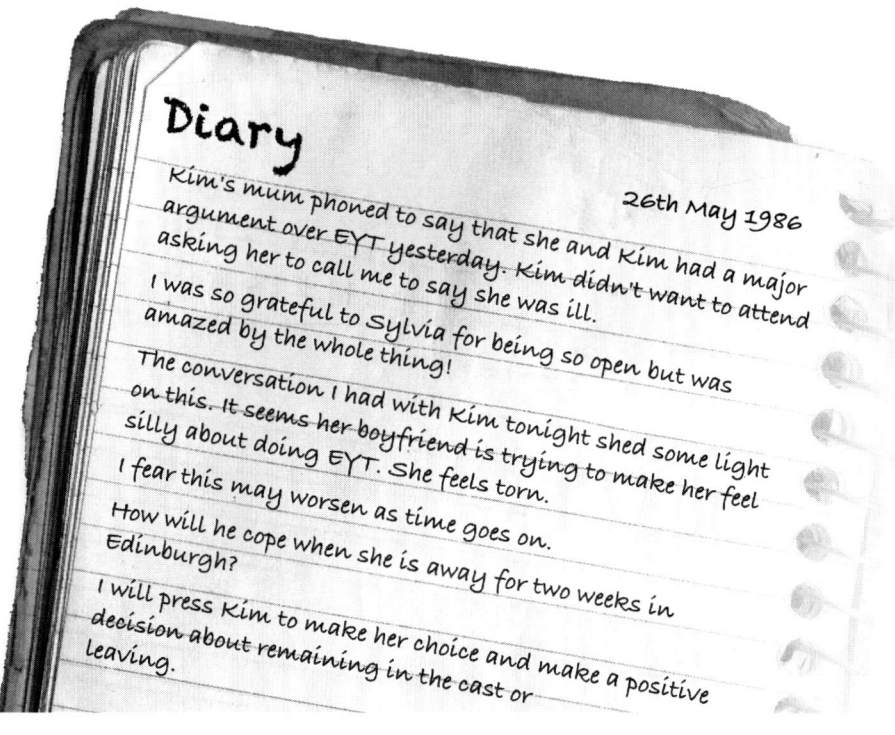

> **Diary**   26th May 1986
>
> Kim's mum phoned to say that she and Kim had a major argument over EYT yesterday. Kim didn't want to attend asking her to call me to say she was ill.
>
> I was so grateful to Sylvia for being so open but was amazed by the whole thing!
>
> The conversation I had with Kim tonight shed some light on this. It seems her boyfriend is trying to make her feel silly about doing EYT. She feels torn.
>
> I fear this may worsen as time goes on. How will he cope when she is away for two weeks in Edinburgh?
>
> I will press Kim to make her choice and make a positive decision about remaining in the cast or leaving.

My optimism was up and down over the next few weeks.

54

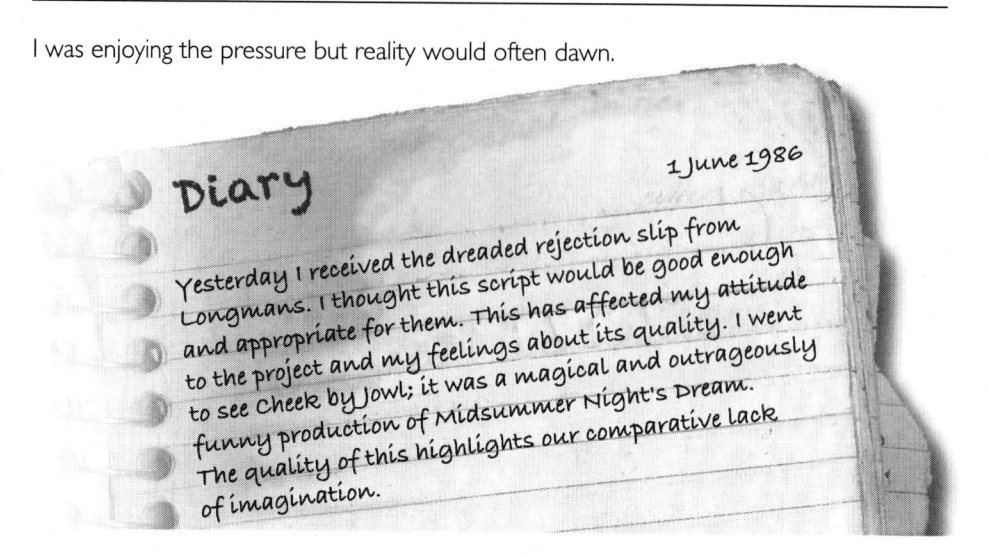

The Story Behind - Too Much Punch For Judy by Mark Wheeller

I was enjoying the pressure but reality would often dawn.

> **Diary**   1 June 1986
>
> Yesterday I received the dreaded rejection slip from Longmans. I thought this script would be good enough and appropriate for them. This has affected my attitude to the project and my feelings about its quality. I went to see Cheek by Jowl; it was a magical and outrageously funny production of Midsummer Night's Dream. The quality of this highlights our comparative lack of imagination.

I was comparing us with the very best in world theatre at the time!

Others were also becoming (some openly) anxious about our progress.

The production mattered, possibly too much. It was all-important and I was protective about it.

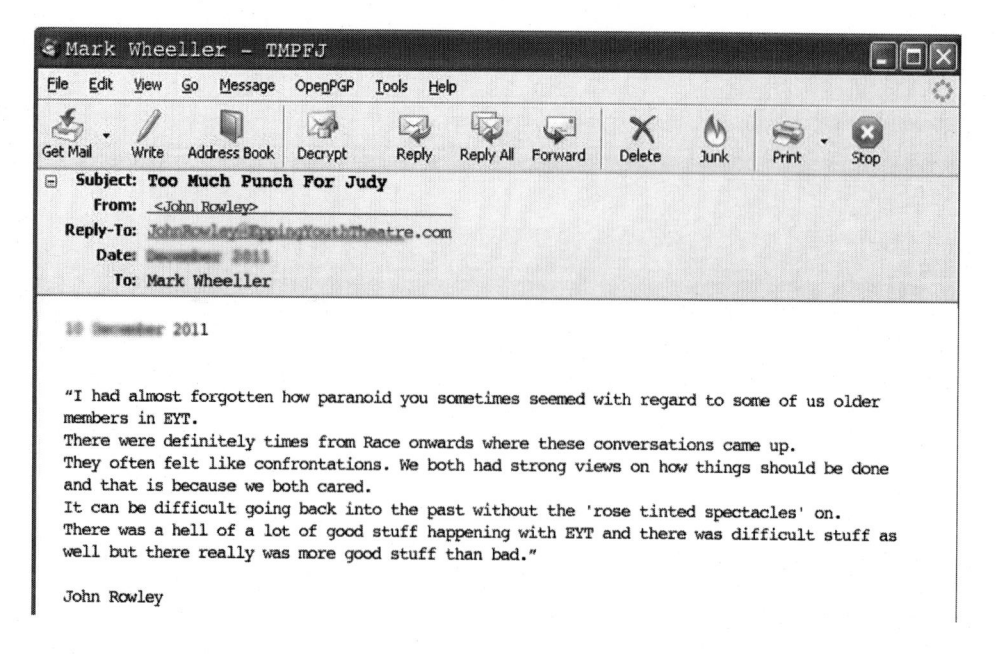

Mark Wheeller - TMPFJ

Subject: Too Much Punch For Judy
From: <John Rowley>
Reply-To: JohnRowley@EppingYouthTheatre.com
Date: December 2011
To: Mark Wheeller

10 December 2011

"I had almost forgotten how paranoid you sometimes seemed with regard to some of us older members in EYT.
There were definitely times from Race onwards where these conversations came up.
They often felt like confrontations. We both had strong views on how things should be done and that is because we both cared.
It can be difficult going back into the past without the 'rose tinted spectacles' on.
There was a hell of a lot of good stuff happening with EYT and there was difficult stuff as well but there really was more good stuff than bad."

John Rowley

The Story Behind - Too Much Punch For Judy by Mark Wheeller

My mood lifted as three sections of "upmarket" folding rostra arrived (Seco Staging). This smart equipment symbolised our achievement and helped us to feel we were doing well!

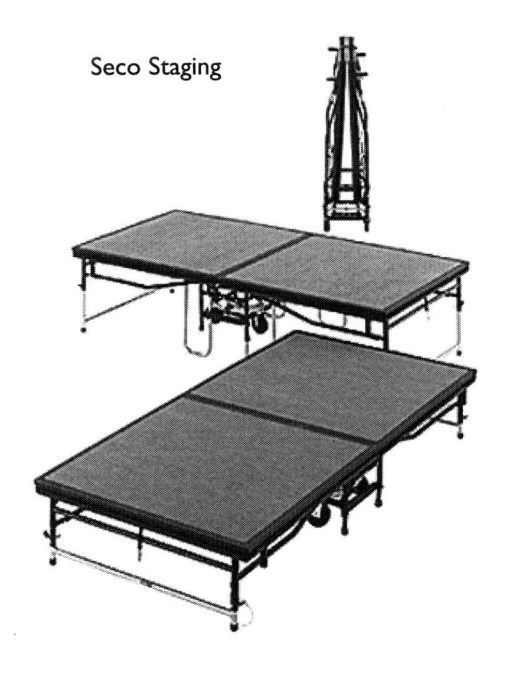

Seco Staging

Mark & Jo 'proud of the new staging'

Diary

"Everything seems to be gelling. I'm feeling supremely confident of the group, the visit to Edinburgh and moreover the play. Ray Cooney has written to me saying he would like to become a patron of EYT.
This is great news and will add to our profile".

A case of non-alcoholic cocktail bottles arrived from the IAS. It was made from two-thirds peach juice and one-third non-alcoholic champagne.

I didn't actually like it but was excited by the novelty of having it at our performances.

---

(17) Ray Cooney OBE is an English playwright and actor who lived in Epping. His biggest success, Run for Your Wife, lasted nine years in the West End and is its longest-running comedy. He has had 17 of his plays performed there to date.

The Story Behind - Too Much Punch For Judy by Mark Wheeller

Once again our work was being upgraded!

John Rowley brought in his incredible poster design.

Quenchers was beginning to take shape!

The Story Behind - Too Much Punch For Judy by Mark Wheeller

Two weeks before the opening performance we suffered a major setback. James Thurber's estate wrote denying us permission for *The Bear Who Couldn't Leave it Alone*.

My reaction was useless but one EYT member, Ryan Gilbey[18], responded more positively and, that same night, drafted out the idea of a King who invented a happiness potion, which had the side effect of death as an allegory to alcohol.

I took his initial idea to one of my drama classes who, in small groups, improvised around it. One group changed the idea of a potion into a bar of soap, washing with it making people happy.

I created a new side effect: body parts disappearing when the soap is overused.

From these ideas, an early version of what became *Wacky Soap* formed to become the penultimate scene in *Quenchers.*

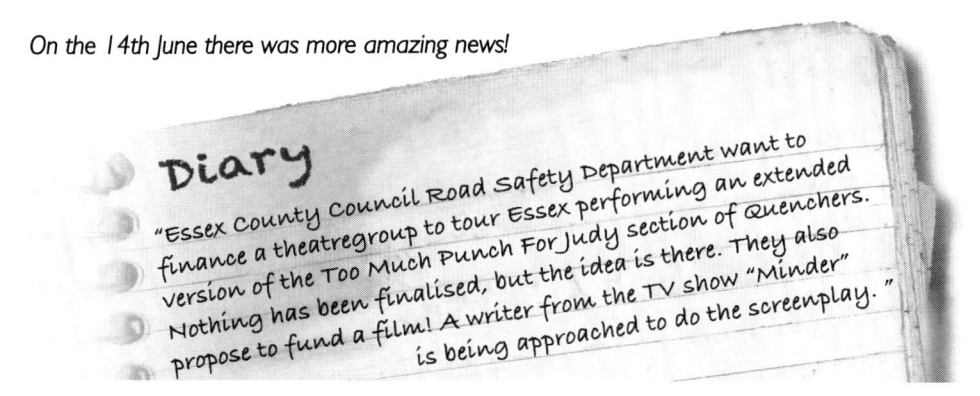

On the 14th June there was more amazing news!

> **Diary**
> "Essex County Council Road Safety Department want to finance a theatregroup to tour Essex performing an extended version of the Too Much Punch For Judy section of Quenchers. Nothing has been finalised, but the idea is there. They also propose to fund a film! A writer from the TV show "Minder" is being approached to do the screenplay."

Reading this now I am amazed at how I was prepared to allow this writer to get in on the act. No extended play existed, let alone a film, but it was then that the idea of extending, what was only a short fifteen-minute scene, into a One Act Play, turned into a plan!

At this time, as luck would have it, Touchstone TIE Company were trying to establish themselves in our region. They had contacted the Essex Drama Advisor, Roger Parsley, (in the days when advisers "advised" rather than inspected or "judged" teachers) to see if he knew of a school, which may be open to the idea of a residency, in return for free rehearsal space. This seemed like an all win deal for both of us and, by this time, we had been working together, developing exciting ideas and a strong bond.

I approached Touchstone with the idea of the TIE tour.

Neither they, nor I, really believed anything would come of it.

---

(18) Ryan has since become a writer well-regarded film critic with the coveted film critic of the year (2007) award to his name.

The Story Behind - Too Much Punch For Judy by Mark Wheeller

Rehearsals, meanwhile, were progressing well.

> **Diary**   14th June 1986:
>
> We rehearsed Judy's arrival at the hospital. Kim was brilliant and particularly sociable tonight! She performs the emotional scenes with such conviction.
>
> Jo and Paul rehearsed the scene where Chris Caten tells mum that Jo was killed. The pauses she and Paul created were full of tension, making it very emotional.
>
> We have no plans for costumes. To be honest, I only thought about that today!

At this juncture I should explain that I ran the Youth Theatre alone, with no support from anyone else. I had to take on responsibility for everything. I had no clue about costumes or lights so it all was left to chance unless a cast member, student in the school or parent suddenly came forward with an expertise… or willingness to help.

The following day (we must have rehearsed a lot!!!) I wrote:

> The hot weather makes me lazy. I worked badly today. Fortunately the imagination and inventiveness of the cast made up for my shortcomings. They were not prepared to accept the first idea, which, I confess, I was. Had they gone with that initial idea I would have returned home unhappy and frustrated with our efforts.

The Story Behind - Too Much Punch For Judy by Mark Wheeller

The *Happy Soap* story (as it was called) was not going well. The Thurber story was short and I was determined the replacement should be no longer.

I felt it was in danger of becoming self-indulgent so took the script the cast were developing home to edit.

The early section of *Quenchers* was also too long so I made edits to that as well.

Although I was still improving *Punch* I was not cutting it at all.

> The second half of tonight's rehearsal focused on Too Much Punch. Kim was outstanding and I went home last night on a high because it was so good. This really is her "moment" I am sure of that! Her mum says she is still getting hassle from her boyfriend. The quality of her work and rewards from that should be a great way of counteracting him!

We had a memorable rehearsal, which, although we didn't know it then, led to an unpredictable series of events:

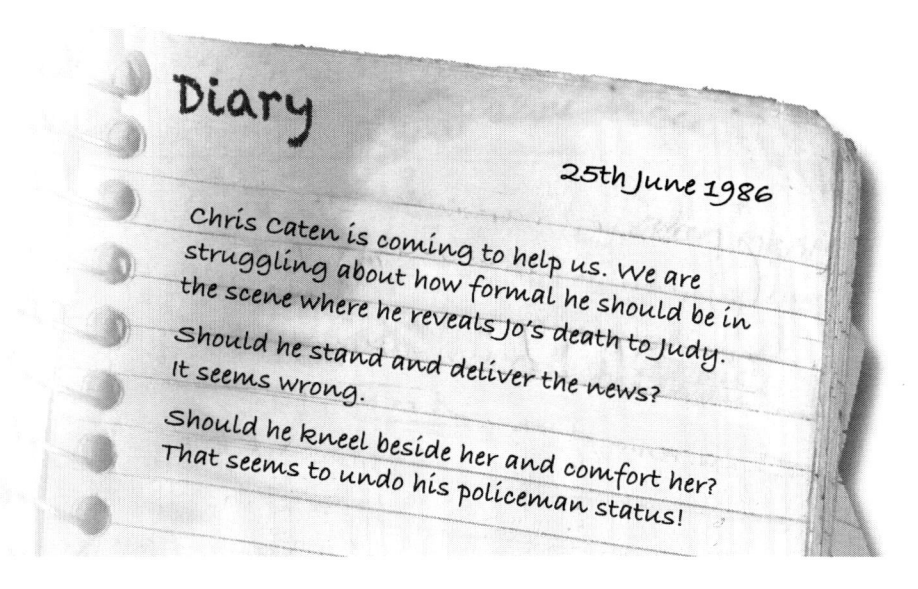

> **Diary**
>
> 25th June 1986
>
> Chris Caten is coming to help us. We are struggling about how formal he should be in the scene where he reveals Jo's death to Judy. Should he stand and deliver the news? It seems wrong.
>
> Should he kneel beside her and comfort her? That seems to undo his policeman status!

The Story Behind - Too Much Punch For Judy by Mark Wheeller

He will hopefully remember what he did and... problem solved!

After that Toni will arrive to see how things are progressing.

This will ensure the cast are on their toes.

I'm very excited and hope no one lets us down over word learning.

An evening not to be missed whatever the outcome!

Post rehearsal Diary entry:

We did ourselves proud.

To resolve the issue of how Chris should convey the news, I asked him to improvise it with Kim playing Toni. This proved incredibly real and spine-tingly. His improvised words were so close to the script Kim was using as her stimulus. He knelt by her wheelchair holding her hands, an incredible input! It must have been an incredible experience for Kim having the real person delivering the news. Wow!

Chris was very impressed by Kim.

Anna also made great progress in her role as Sister Davis.

Toni commented afterwards how similar she was to her memory of the real nurse.

Having the real people in to see our work raises the game for our cast. They have reached performance standard two weeks prior to the production.

Normally, in my productions, things only come together in the final week of rehearsals.

Page to Stage

The Story Behind - Too Much Punch For Judy by Mark Wheeller

Kim hadn't said anything to me but it came to light that she had found this rehearsal compromising. Chris had recently arrested her boyfriend who was up on a serious charge. It had proved an impossible rehearsal for her. None of us (including her parents) knew anything about this at the time, and I didn't find out for a long while, so what happened next came as a complete shock to all of us and seemed inexplicable.

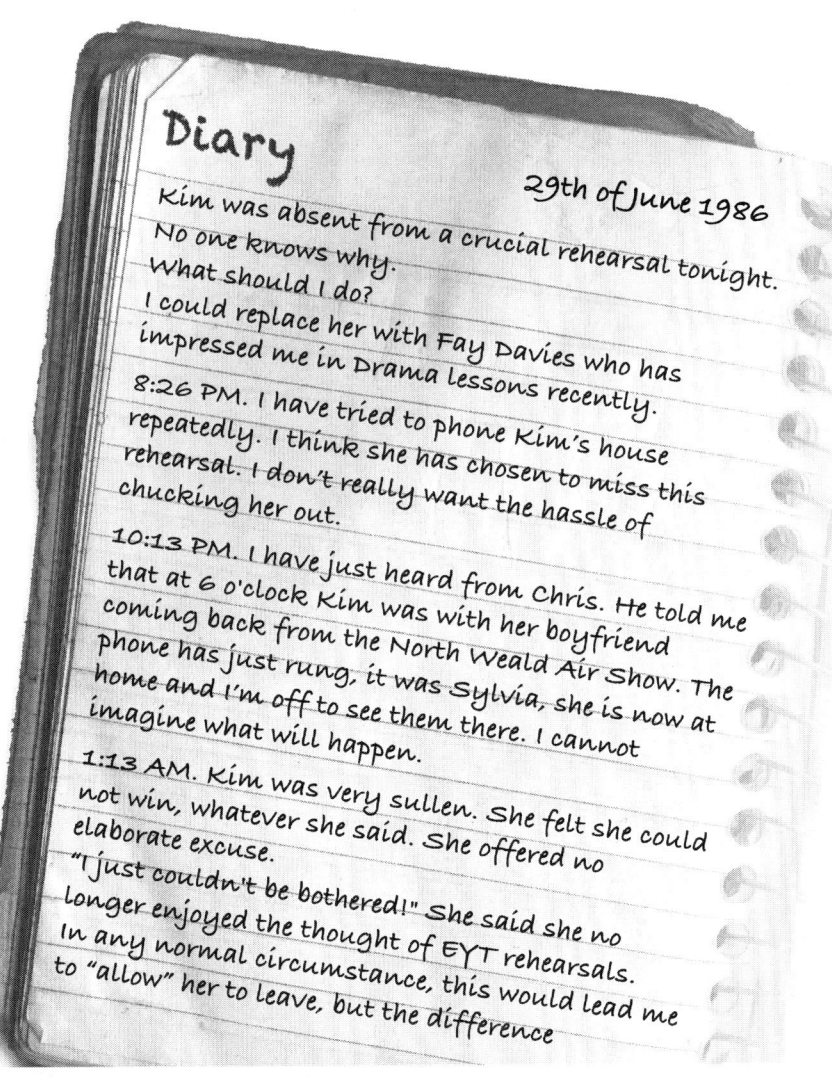

Diary
29th of June 1986

Kim was absent from a crucial rehearsal tonight. No one knows why. What should I do? I could replace her with Fay Davies who has impressed me in Drama lessons recently.

8:26 PM. I have tried to phone Kim's house repeatedly. I think she has chosen to miss this rehearsal. I don't really want the hassle of chucking her out.

10:13 PM. I have just heard from Chris. He told me that at 6 o'clock Kim was with her boyfriend coming back from the North Weald Air Show. The phone has just rung, it was Sylvia, she is now at home and I'm off to see them there. I cannot imagine what will happen.

1:13 AM. Kim was very sullen. She felt she could not win, whatever she said. She offered no elaborate excuse.

"I just couldn't be bothered!" She said she no longer enjoyed the thought of EYT rehearsals. In any normal circumstance, this would lead me to "allow" her to leave, but the difference

The Story Behind - Too Much Punch For Judy by Mark Wheeller

here is the enthusiasm of her parents, who think she has too much to lose jacking it in. We talked for ages, Kim going to bed about midnight. The ensuing conversation with her mum and dad was more encouraging. They offered all the support I could want or need. Tomorrow, Kim will see me in the afternoon to let me know what she decides to do.

30th of June 1986

Kim dropped out at 3:25pm.

By 3:30pm I'd cast Fay Davies and will work with her from 6 tonight. It will be hard but I have every confidence in her. She cried when I asked and hasn't stopped talking about it since, according to her mum!

Kim phoned me at 5:30 to say she now realises she's made the wrong decision... but... she has made that decision.

I wonder if she is taking on this attitude to pacify her mum and dad.

I hope I can report good things on my return from rehearsal. I hope the others will turn up to rehearse with Fay. I have no idea how they will react to all of this!

The Story Behind - Too Much Punch For Judy by Mark Wheeller

Fay

It seems very understated to say merely that I replaced Kim with Fay just four days before the first performance. We had all been working on this for over a year. Kim was perfect for the role and was all set to be the star of the piece! Suddenly, our trump card had dropped out.

This main role now rested with someone who had done nothing towards the preparation of the play. Moreover she was in the 4th year (Year 10). She would be one of the youngest in the cast.

She had been a dancer in EYT's *Joseph and his Amazing Technicolor* and played a small role in our (poor) version of *Gregory's Girl*.

She had been impressive in school Drama classes (I'd been teaching her since the start of that year) and had lots of enthusism, but if I had been that impressed, why hadn't I encouraged her to become involved in the project prior to this?

I could have offered the role to someone in the cast although but no one was particularly well suited to it. Not only that but I would have had to replace the role(s) they vacated making the situation even more complex.

> *"I jumped at the chance to play this part. It was a biggie involving a trip to the Edinburgh Festival! I was only 15 and the chance of a "lead role" telling such a sensitive story of "real life" people (we're not talking Bugsy Malone here!) was like winning the lottery. It was a challenge but I knew I could do it! I only had four days to learn the script. I remember school gave me time off, so I sat in my back garden learning the lines! I remember feeling like a celebrity, after the Thames at Six news feature!*

The Story Behind - Too Much Punch For Judy by Mark Wheeller

> "Although I met Toni a couple of times, I played the part as if it were me. I reacted as I would in that situation. Mark talked about this way of approaching a role when we worked in Drama lessons so I applied that to this performance. I had nothing in common with Toni at all as she was much more streetwise.
> I feared the cast might be upset that I had come in and taken the lead role only four days before a performance as they had all put in a lot of work researching etc. but they all came in for extra rehearsals to help me."
> **Fay Davies (2011)**

I remember being excited, hoping the disruption would serve to focus everyone, renew energies and encourage the cast to work even harder!

My Post Rehearsal Diary entry:

> **Diary**
> Fay worked very well and has begun to make the part her own. I called her Kim by mistake once – woops! She is more emotional in her portrayal but less aggressive. When Paul and John arrived there was some tension. They felt uneasy, saying it seemed sad that yesterday Kim was involved and today she isn't.

There really has been no time to explain to any of them the details of what had happened so they had to just get on with it. I guess they could have felt I was hiding things. They only had my side of the story. These days people would have been texting or Facebooking each other but in 1986 this wasn't possible. I doubt many would have even known Kim's home phone number (landline).

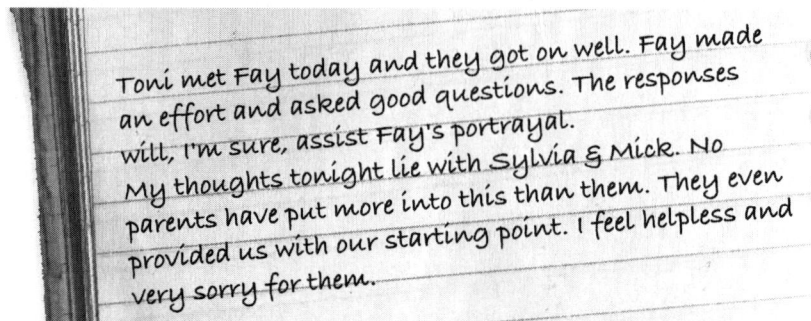

> Toni met Fay today and they got on well. Fay made an effort and asked good questions. The responses will, I'm sure, assist Fay's portrayal.
> My thoughts tonight lie with Sylvia & Mick. No parents have put more into this than them. They even provided us with our starting point. I feel helpless and very sorry for them.

The Story Behind - Too Much Punch For Judy by Mark Wheeller

2 July 1986 (The day before the preview performance)

I'm so tired and can hardly stay up to write this. Yesterday's rehearsal was a happy affair; everyone worked hard in the most relaxed of situations. I hardly made any correction notes at all. Sylvia and Mick have been very big and came down to speak to everyone. They brought a letter from Kim:

Dear Mark and Youth Theatre,

At the moment I cannot bring myself to speak to you personally. I know there aren't any bad feelings and I don't have any towards you. However, I feel I owe the Youth Theatre (my friends) an explanation and an apology. The Sunday I did not turn up for the rehearsal. It wasn't anything personal, I just felt a bit down with Youth Theatre. I'd like to apologise as I have let you all down. That evening Mark came round and I was unable to give him any good reasons for not attending as there weren't any. We decided to sleep on it and I would see him the next day, which I did. I made a hasty decision because I didn't have time to think it over. I realise this was the wrong decision but I don't blame you Mark, I blame myself and respect your decision to re-cast my part. I do not hold any grudges against you or Fay as I think she will be good. It was my decision. Mark, I wish you and EYT all the success it deserves on such a worthwhile project.

Thanks to all of you and don't lose touch.

Good luck and all the best.

Thanks a million

Kim x

The Story Behind - Too Much Punch For Judy by Mark Wheeller

Kim's letter was really helpful to diffuse any residual tensions and I was so grateful to Sylvia and Mick for coming down to see us personally.

Fay's attempts at the long speeches were initially no match for Kim's but as the evening progressed she improved. I think she will get good reviews just as Kim would have done.

The funniest moment of the evening was when John Rowley had to pick Fay up (Duncan pulling Toni out from the wreckage of the car). Twice he was forced to fart with the effort of the lift. An expectation that he would do this the third time meant it took ages for us to be able to cope with re-running this scene.

This run through was excellent... considering. I think Too Much Punch alone is impressive. We will have to see whether the rest of the play detracts too much. I look forward to the reaction we get tomorrow.
Fay has a golden opportunity.

The Story Behind - Too Much Punch For Judy by Mark Wheeller

John Rowley and Fay – the scene that made him fart!

3 July 1986 (Preview Performance Day)

4.41 in the morning.

I can't sleep.

I am worried about the audience tonight. How many will come?

During the day I must attempt to boost the numbers or else we could well end up with less than 10!

I keep thinking of Fay who has started to develop a cold! Will she have learnt her lines?

Should we have a prompt (we never had in previous productions)?

The Story Behind - Too Much Punch For Judy by Mark Wheeller

8.00am

Eventually I got back to bed and had an entertaining nightmare:

We were (surprise, surprise) performing the play in front of and "invited to be critical" audience in the hall with and impressively big scaffolding set. The opening scene was brand-new. I knew nothing about it! Paul made a mistake and started murmuring his words under his breath! I shouted at him- and used the 'F' word in public. Doing that, woke me up!

4:20pm

Of all days, I was grabbed to cover this afternoon! I could have done without that.

I have not managed to organise a blanket for Fay when she's in the wheelchair.

I'm not quite sure how the cast will manage some major costume changes in the confines of the drama room. This is something I've completely overlooked. I must now make up the second tape, then shove some food down and get on back to school to meet Fay at 5.30pm for a final word run. Here goes!!!

The Story Behind - Too Much Punch For Judy by Mark Wheeller

4. Quenchers - First Performance

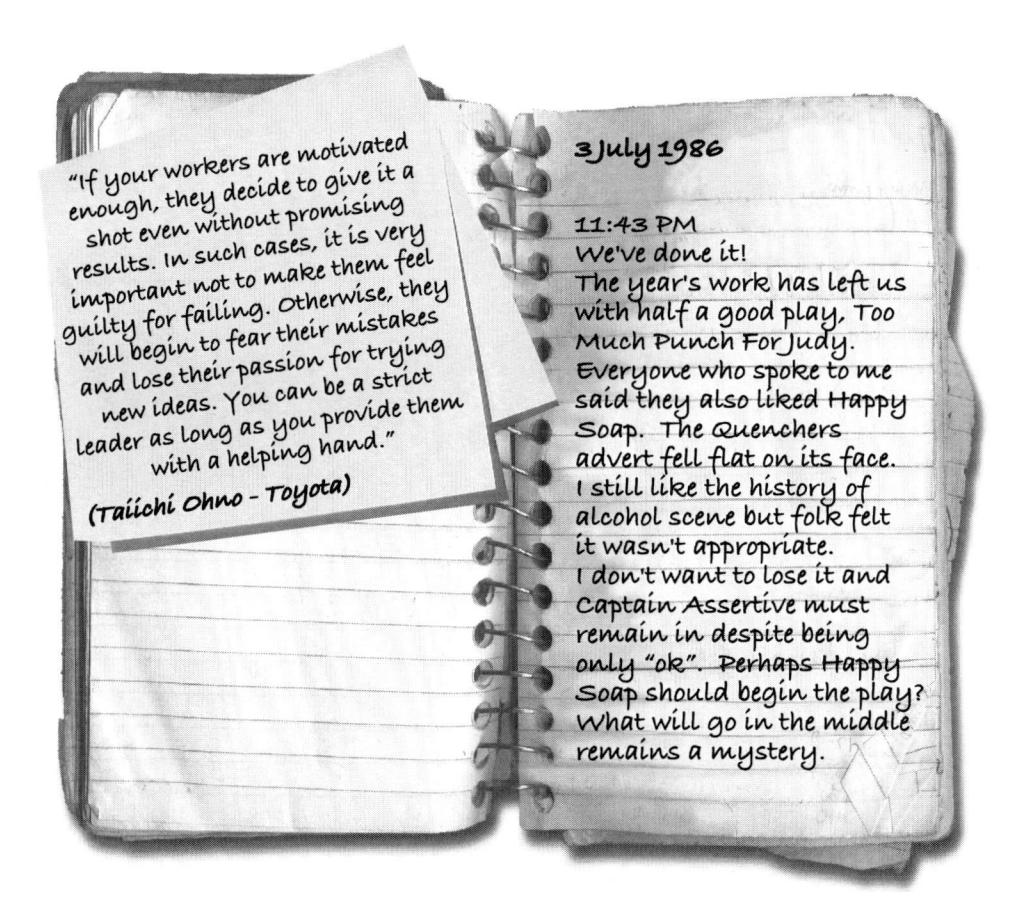

"If your workers are motivated enough, they decide to give it a shot even without promising results. In such cases, it is very important not to make them feel guilty for failing. Otherwise, they will begin to fear their mistakes and lose their passion for trying new ideas. You can be a strict leader as long as you provide them with a helping hand."

(Taiichi Ohno - Toyota)

3 July 1986

11:43 PM
We've done it!
The year's work has left us with half a good play, Too Much Punch For Judy. Everyone who spoke to me said they also liked Happy Soap. The Quenchers advert fell flat on its face. I still like the history of alcohol scene but folk felt it wasn't appropriate. I don't want to lose it and Captain Assertive must remain in despite being only "ok". Perhaps Happy Soap should begin the play? What will go in the middle remains a mystery.

We met to do a re-write based on the feedback we received. The official premiere was scheduled the following week at the prestigious (for us) Harlow Playhouse Studio Theatre. From reading my diary, we made some significant alterations but, once again, none to the *Punch* section.

The Story Behind - Too Much Punch For Judy by Mark Wheeller

What thrills me more than anything else was the commitment the cast had to working on these changes. They dropped what they were doing to help sort it. This is really impressive. Paul was bubbling over with ideas! On the 8th July Thames at Six recorded a promotional news item[19] that made us feel we are doing something very exciting. We went onto our dress rehearsal where I realised I'd made a basic planning error.

I have not staged it for 3 sides, which is how Harlow Playhouse Studio Theatre is laid out. Why didn't I think of this before? Lots of changes had to be made. The dress rehearsal lasted over one and a half hours. The order is still not right. I'm tempted to write a note to the audience to explain our predicament. Some of it seemed decidedly amateur, even Punch. I hope an audience will pick people up a bit.

9th July 1986
Our first "public performance" was a success, very much a company effort.
Too Much Punch was good although Fay's performance was too restrained. The cuts we made last week helped and there is not much I want to change...

---

(19) This can still be seen on YouTube if you search Too Much Punch For Judy

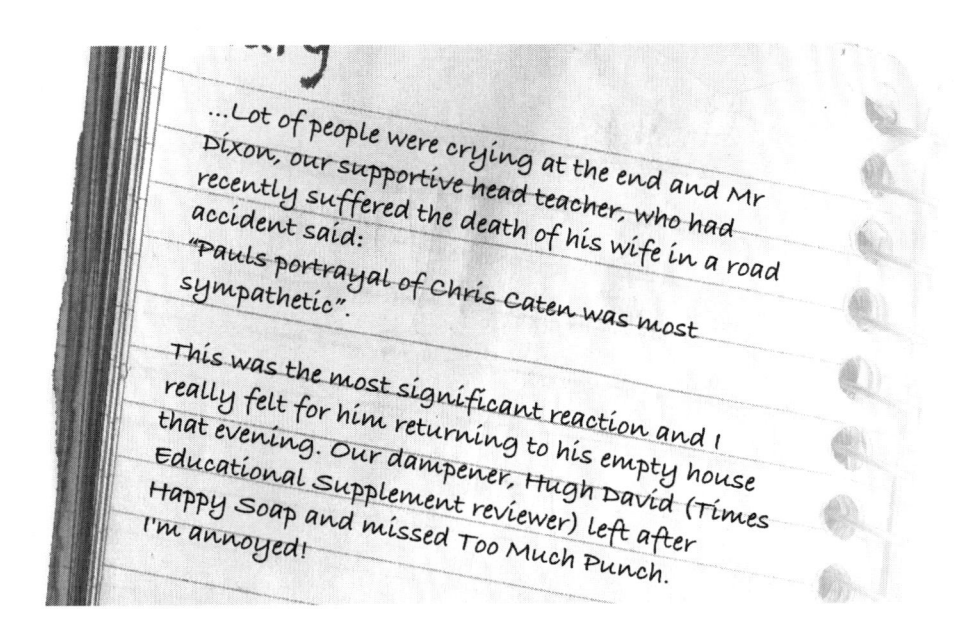

The Story Behind - Too Much Punch For Judy by Mark Wheeller

> ...Lot of people were crying at the end and Mr Dixon, our supportive head teacher, who had recently suffered the death of his wife in a road accident said:
> "Pauls portrayal of Chris Caten was most sympathetic".
>
> This was the most significant reaction and I really felt for him returning to his empty house that evening. Our dampener, Hugh David (Times Educational Supplement reviewer) left after Happy Soap and missed Too Much Punch. I'm annoyed!

I was indebted to Hugh for attending our productions and reviewing them for such a prestigious newspaper. However, he *always* left at the interval. In this play, there was no interval so I thought he would stay for the whole performance. I hadn't realised at the time, he was paid to do these reviews. I only questioned his actions recently when I saw an article about reviewer's ethics:

> *"Critics are required to sit through whatever is thrown at them, be it shocking, preposterous, dreadful or dull."*
> **Guardian Arts; Culture Walk Outs: Our Critics Take. 25.10.2011**

I asked Ryan Gilbey, a cast member at the time and now a highly respected film critic.

> *"That's scandalous! The first rule of criticism has to be: You stay for the whole thing otherwise you have lost the right to review. It's dereliction of duty and it makes me so cross. I'm shocked and retrospectively angry with the TES for that - especially as the second half of Quenchers puts the first into context. Imagine a rock critic only reviewing the first side of Ziggy! It renders his review invalid."*

It seems Ryan's is a well-established view:

> *"I don't do walk outs, partly out of professional ethics and partly because I don't like making a spectacle of my displeasure."*
> **Brian Logan; Comedy critic. Guardian Arts; Culture Walk Outs: Our Critics Take. 25.10.2011**

The Story Behind - Too Much Punch For Judy by Mark Wheeller

On this occasion, I was particularly frustrated because Hugh missed what was, I felt, the high point of our performance. He missed it, not through disapproval of what we were doing but out of what I perceived to be laziness! We had previously benefitted from favourable reviews of the half-productions he had seen and I had never complained to the TES because I feared we might lose the chance of future reviews. At least in those days they reviewed school productions; now they don't. I was sufficiently annoyed by his early departure that I sneaked out to ask him why he was leaving. His response was that he was worried he would miss the train! It was only about 8.15! Harlow wasn't a little village. *Grrr!*

His review of *Quenchers* was the only review of the play that omitted *Too Much Punch*, so in that respect, it is of historical interest but I would have been interested to read his opinion of the whole play.

> These days every play is seemingly loaded with statistics. They were about all there was in Epping Youth Theatre's anti-booze play Quenchers. Play? No, in this case that is something of a misnomer.
>
> The piece was more an old-fashioned temperance rally given the youth theatre treatment. T-shirts and rostra blocks could not conceal the fact that although the research had been done, it had not been fully digested. There were some interesting thoughts about drink from young children but, like the testimonies of members of Alcoholics Anonymous, they were delivered skilfully, but straight out front, verbatim. It was a worthy, but still rather surprising production. Is alcohol really such a problem out there in Harlow? Surely not.
>
> Leaving the Playhouse studio after the show, just in time for a final bevvy, I couldn't even find a pub.
>
> **Hugh David - Times Educational Supplement.**

He even had time to look around for a pub before his train?!? Thanks Hugh!
The second night's performance dipped with cast arriving late and frustrating me with ill discipline on stage.

The Story Behind - Too Much Punch For Judy by Mark Wheeller

The most memorable aspect of that night was afterwards as Toni met the real Duncan. Chris Caten came over and said,

"Toni, I've got a friend of yours here"
"A friend?"
"Yes. Duncan Wick."

She nearly exploded! They obviously felt quite awkward meeting for the first time since he'd dragged her from the car to prevent her from returning to it, but they chatted, albeit awkwardly, for a while.

I was intrigued to hear how Toni reacted to being in the audience and, when I later interviewed her for the introduction to the play script, she told me:

"I breezed through getting ready. I breezed into Harlow Playhouse, got into the Theatre and then nearly lost control.
I was flinching all the time. It made me sweat trying not to lose control.
I didn't know whether to cry and walk out or be sick and walk out.
I remember there were some young blokes, about eighteen, across from us and they were crying. I was surprised. I never thought it would upset people like that, I really didn't."

Toni.

I noted in my diary that for our final Harlow performance everyone was excellent and there were no technical hitches!

Kim's brother came with his mum and dad and became upset during the story set in his house. We presented them with a six-bottle case of non-alcoholic champagne. It was so supportive of them to come and they seemed to enjoy it.

In the days that followed, people spoke highly of the production. The following week we awaited the publication of the local reviews. The first was from the *West Essex, Epping Gazette* (who would go on to be lifelong supporters of the play) and was published on the 15th July.

The Story Behind - Too Much Punch For Judy by Mark Wheeller

West Essex (Epping Gazette)

THEATRE REVIEW

Spilling it all Out... Quenchers. It goes to your head like pure spirit, but leaves you stone cold sober. Epping Youth Theatre hit the bottle hard for their new play. One scene after another brought out characters whose worst enemies stirred up from the bottom of the glass... The play's climax was the true story of the death of local girl Jo... Fay Davies turned in a brilliant performance as Toni. PC Chris Caten praised it as being "realistic and disturbing".

Gillian Crawley – West Essex (Epping Gazette)

The Amateur Stage review came out soon after:

REVIEWS

"It makes its impact with some style and punch, particularly in the final episode, which is based on a local fatal accident as seen through the words of those involved and immediately affected. With the exception of Fay Davies, who plays the killer driver in the last scene, one is not struck by the quality of individual performances—but this is a company show and needs to be."

Roger Parsley: Amateur Stage

The Story Behind - Too Much Punch For Judy by Mark Wheeller

On the 17th July we tried to improve our simple staging of the accident scene. I had started to realise more was possible:

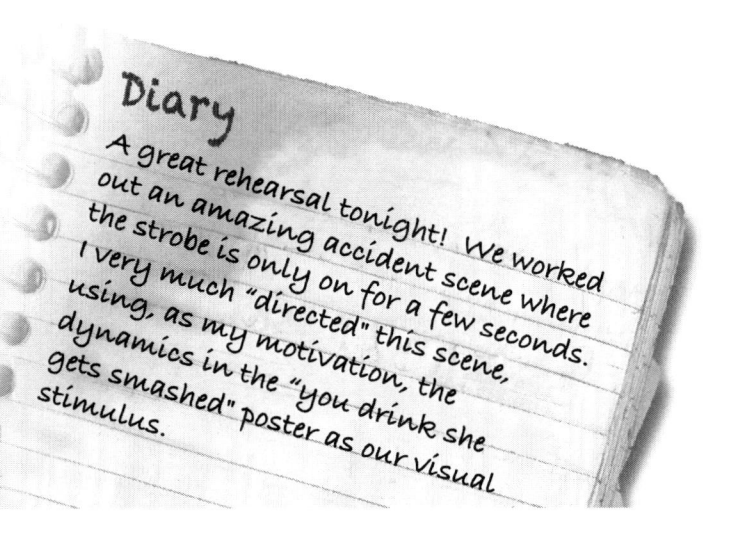

Diary

A great rehearsal tonight! We worked out an amazing accident scene where the strobe is only on for a few seconds. I very much "directed" this scene, using, as my motivation, the dynamics in the "you drink she gets smashed" poster as our visual stimulus.

The Story Behind - Too Much Punch For Judy by Mark Wheeller

I didn't write more in my diary but I think this scene would have had some fast movement in it to make the strobe effective as I know I always used large and fast physical actions when a strobe was on. I suspect this was the impetus to make the scene more physical. I know I encouraged the actor playing Jo to hurl herself forward at a given time and end in the freeze depicted in the image above.

Page to Stage

David from (Essex) Road Safety came to watch this rehearsal and was impressed. He brought a transcript of a glowing review, which was heading for a national road safety Newsletter.

NEWSLETTER

London Borough of Redbridge
DG Harrington Road Safety Officer

FOCUS !

Road Safety

Drinking & Driving Kills

"I went to see the play to view it objectively as a professional Road Safety Officer but readily confess that the dramatic effects on the family of the fatally injured girl, so vividly portrayed, affected me personally as a father of two daughters and a son – all car drivers. I've yet to see a more dramatic approach to the problems of drinking and driving and would certainly like the opportunity for drivers of all ages, let alone teenage drivers, to see the treatment given to this subject by the Epping Youth Theatre"

We had been noticed !

Our next stop was the Edinburgh Festival Fringe where I was more anxious about being responsible for this group of young people than about the performance. No one was giving me any particular cause for concern but I was not much older than my charges and the only teacher on the trip! That would not be allowed these days. None of the staff at my school expressed interest in assisting so I took an ex-Stantonbury Youth Theatre member, Shahnaz Hussain, who became our female "responsible adult" aged only 22. She had met the group once and had only infrequent contact with me since I moved from Milton Keynes.

Everyone was positive about the prospect of the trip and full of hopes and dreams about how it might go… and me? I was banking on a Fringe First!

The Story Behind - Too Much Punch For Judy by Mark Wheeller

Diary 31st July 1986:

I'm finally experiencing the excitement I expected to feel during the Harlow performances. I've bought a frame for the cast picture that will from now sit on my TV. It shows the close-knit nature of this group and how they have, in many ways been my substitute family. Like all families, it will eventually go its separate ways. It is my hope that we will remain in contact and continue to honour this piece of work we've made. It certainly feels, after the previews, that we are now off to do the performances proper!

The Quenchers Cast

Back row left to right: Paul Elliott; Emma Turner; Jon Ward; Jo (Unicorn) Redman; Gus Shield; Mark Wheeller
Middle Row left to right: Nick Fradd; Barrie Sapsford; John Rowley; Ryan Gilbey; Fay Davies.
Front Row left to right: Debbie Pollard; Anna Wallbank; Jo Dumelow; Nicole Redman.

The Story Behind - Too Much Punch For Judy by Mark Wheeller

5. Quenchers - on the Edinburgh Fringe.

The Edinburgh Festival (Fringe) is the world's largest Arts Festival. Buildings become Theatres hosting multiple productions. Streets become performance areas and groups are everywhere leafleting. Tickets are hard to sell unless your product (and/or your publicity machine) is very good.

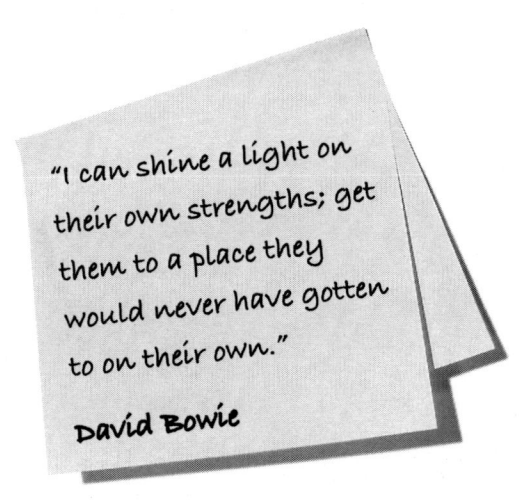

> *"I can shine a light on their own strengths; get them to a place they would never have gotten to on their own."*
>
> David Bowie

* In 2011 there were 2,542 different shows in the four weeks of the festival [20]
* I remember the figure was something in the region of 1,800 (in three weeks) in 1986 and that the average audience attendance was 8.5 people
* The Festival is open access. There is no quality control. Anyone can participate as long as you can afford to pay for the various associated costs.

Performing at the Fringe offered credibility for what we were doing. Once there, we would battle with professionals for punters to put their hands in their pockets. It was never going to be easy, but there were other youth groups there and we hoped to attract some of them.

---

(20) Source www.edfringe.com

The Story Behind - Too Much Punch For Judy by Mark Wheeller

Our cast (aged from 14-19) travelled by coach (some of the older ones) and train (with Shahnaz). I took the three youngest by car (an 850cc Renault 4!).

I remember vividly how excited I was when we met at Edinburgh station and ran (yes I could run in those days!) up to greet them. We all felt something special was about to happen!

In the first week we had the run of Bill's Royal Blind School in Edinburgh, as the students weren't back from their summer holidays. We used the School Hall in the mornings to create Street Theatre adverts for our production, to rehearse and for workshops. This allowed us to be creative (more often than not, funny) and enjoy ourselves inexpensively. We spent time on the Royal Mile doing Street Theatre, leafleting and offering people *Quenchers* drinks, which proved to be a unique gimmick. The first day we did a very quick "get in" and the following day our Edinburgh Premiere.

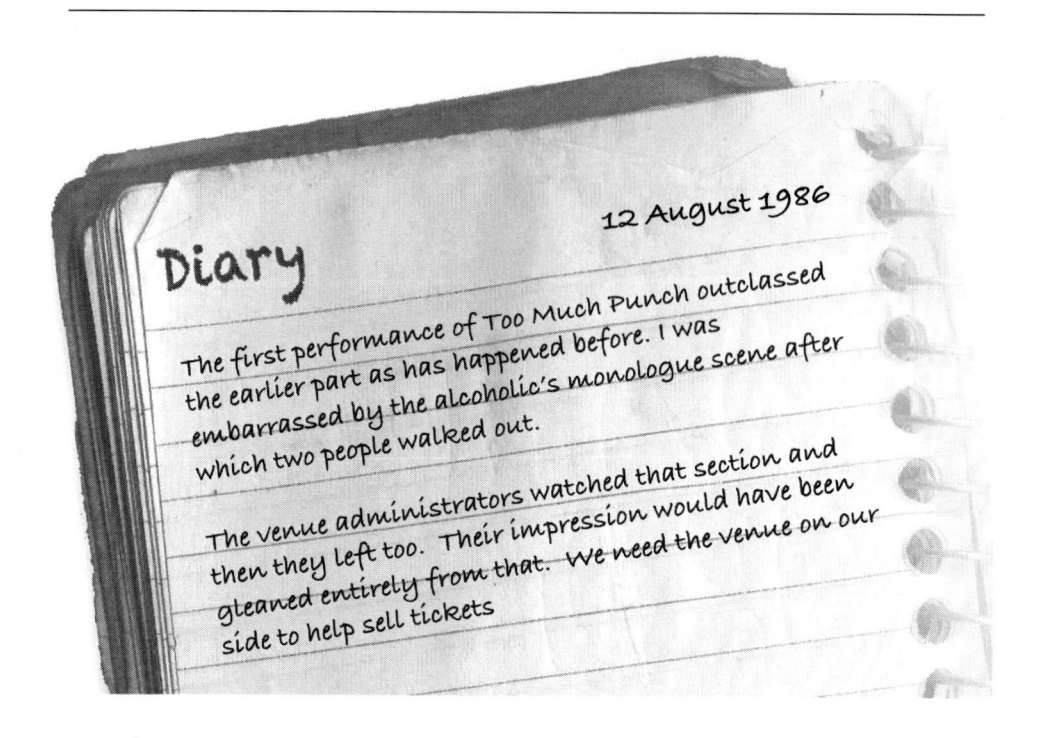

The Story Behind - Too Much Punch For Judy by Mark Wheeller

> **Diary**   12 August 1986
>
> The first performance of Too Much Punch outclassed the earlier part as has happened before. I was embarrassed by the alcoholic's monologue scene after which two people walked out.
>
> The venue administrators watched that section and then they left too. Their impression would have been gleaned entirely from that. We need the venue on our side to help sell tickets

Everyone in the cast was aware of the people who walked out and so knew things were not going as well as we hoped. My reaction, typically, was to suggest a massive cut which, if it were agreed to, would deny one cast member (Jon, as Dave the pop star) his main role. It proved impossible to balance artistic integrity with sensitivity to the group. It fell to me to cause the first upset.

My suggestion to cut his scene led to much bad feeling. Finally the cast agreed and stayed up late to do another rewrite, but also protect Jon, who was one of the youngest cast members.

The following morning we staged the new script and re-jigged the casting. The amendments resulted in cuts of nearly 7 minutes! The group effort paid off, kept the play fresh and everyone more motivated for the afternoon's performance. My risky strategy paid off!

I wrote in my diary that I really wanted **The Scotsman** to see it that night and, as luck would have it, they did. The reviewer was generous in her laughter and, unlike Hugh David, stayed to see the whole production! The tenor of her review could influence our success on the Fringe.

The Story Behind - Too Much Punch For Judy by Mark Wheeller

REVIEWS

"The show is performed in documentary style... a mixture of dramatised quotes and comments and improvisations... some of the bits work extremely well. Most successful, often movingly so, are the scenes which use actual incidents and the words actually used to describe them; they need no embellishment, wisely received none and are the more effective for it. Fay Davies turns in a most poignant performance in the final scene... a formidable attack on alcohol abuse generally and on drunken driving particularly."
Pru Kitching the Scotsman Friday, August 15, 1986

I didn't record in my diary anything about the review from the Scotsman; probably because, although not a disaster, it had become obvious we would not win a Fringe First (an award, that despite several attempts, still eludes me!). Re-reading this review now I realise it is good, but at the time, I was disappointed, feeling that only *Too Much Punch* came out well!

It was thrilling to arrive at the ticket office each morning to discover the level of ticket sales. Anything in double figures gave us cause for excitement. We were attracting over 20 for most performances and on one occasion, nearly 50.

The ensuing performances continued to improve but for the first time I began to feel changes were needed in the *Too Much Punch* section.

The Story Behind - Too Much Punch For Judy by Mark Wheeller

> **Diary**
>
> Tonight I plan to make a change to Too Much Punch by putting the hospital scene after Vi hears the news from Chris Caten to add pace. This should perhaps be the final scene as Duncan's final speech (about clearing up the debris) de-focuses the message or... yes this is a good idea... Toni should close the show, saying how she will never drink and drive again?

The following day we were thrown into a crisis with our venue for Week 2.

I visited to check it out and discovered to my horror they had a solid construction in the middle of the stage. I assumed they would clear it by the second week but enquired, just to be on the safe side. The team at the venue told us it was there for the duration of the Festival. There was no way *Quenchers* could be performed on this small stage with an erection in the middle! I couldn't imagine many plays that could. I remained confident that they would find a way round it. They didn't!

We were forced to search for another venue (at this very late stage) and became embroiled in a fight for a full refund to pay for a replacement venue! (Had we not been in Edinburgh we would never have known about this until our arrival.) The Fringe Office became involved on our behalf and, after much stress, we received the refund and found another venue. However, this was not an entirely happy ending! We had to use our limited box office income to re-print all our publicity leaflets. We received no compensation for the expensive adverts in the Fringe program, advertising our performances at the original venue and at a different time!

It was a setback but, much like the Kim situation four days before our first Harlow performance, it fired us up!

Our audiences for the second week were often in single figures. We gave tickets away for the final performance to create a decent sized audience. Even so we were nowhere near putting up the "House Full" signs.

A highlight of our visit for me was when John and Paul drew a massive chalk *Quenchers* poster on the pavement near the Fringe Box Office on the final day, which attracted a lot of interest.

The Story Behind - Too Much Punch For Judy by Mark Wheeller

The Quenchers Cast promoting the play in Edinburgh

Although not a hit, *Quenchers* had been presented at the *Edinburgh Fringe* and, so too had a small part of what would become *Too Much Punch For Judy* offering it some early credibility.

On my return to Epping I wrote in my diary (headlined "Final Entry") a typically sentimental piece about the end of the production. Although by no means a failure, *Quenchers* hadn't been the massive success I'd imagined it would be.

84

The Story Behind - Too Much Punch For Judy by Mark Wheeller

Diary

Monday 25th of August FINAL ENTRY.

The audience on the last night (as they were on the first) were somewhat flat but became more intent during Too Much Punch. The performance was good and the cast gained a well-deserved elongated applause at the end.

On 30 September last year, with the exception of Kim, I was the first to arrive at the initial meeting to start our work on an unnamed play about alcohol misuse. Yesterday I was the last to return home, (Kim no longer involved) arriving 13 hours after our departure from Edinburgh.

We had performed Quencher, the play we had worked so hard to create twelve times there. The excitement of the new beginnings has become the warm satisfaction of success and the "romance of happy family atmosphere in Edinburgh. In bed that night I dreamt about Edinburgh or the people who were involved in the trip. One perhaps is allegorical of the "end" of Quenchers. Here it is:

John Rowley and I were walking by Centrepoint in St John's Road where we held many of our rehearsals. Suddenly up above us we saw an inflatable rubber dinghy with a propeller at the back attached to the engine. The engine had caught fire and was swooping down towards Centrepoint. John ran towards the fire station. I told the fireman who, it transpired, had already been alerted. I woke up. I wonder if anything from Centrepoint was salvaged. In the real world I wonder whether I can salvage anything from Quenchers?

On arriving at my house, one of the first things I saw was the picture of the cast, taken two days before our Harlow performance on my TV. Everyone looked happy and reminded me of the experiences, that we all had the opportunity to share. I felt a strange mixture of feelings: joyous, satisfied, proud, and contented. The next moment it hit me. Quenchers was over and now becomes a glorious memory, a tremendous achievement, and... yes, I've done it... a soppy end to this diary!

85

The Story Behind - Too Much Punch For Judy by Mark Wheeller

6. Too Much Punch For Judy -
EYT Rehearsals.

> I try to find ways of (survival strategy?) raising the status of any project I am involved in beyond its real status. I attach an importance to it, which my cast and I metaphorically sign up to thus making it essential that it is completed! It instigates an approach to new ventures with a naïve (over)-confidence and forces us to take creative/artistic risks. I think these days I am more consciously aware of this as a strategy. At this stage it was pure instinct. It certainly motivates my groups.

> *"The time has come for this form of Theatre to penetrate schools and communities everywhere. The motto is "Dig where you stand". Every square foot of England has a stage full of actors, designers, etc. to do justice to it."*
>
> Roy Nevitt – Director of The Living Archive Project.

I had no intention of adding anything to my production diary. *Quenchers* was complete.

Too Much Punch was a different project and, as far as EYT was concerned, an unexpected side project! I had already committed to staging *Oliver!* (my favourite musical at the time) during the autumn term but, sadly, that became frustrating, hardly surprising given that the "side project" took up so much more of my time.

Early in the New Year, with *Oliver!* behind me I returned to write in my production diary:

I have included this reference to my own (private) arrogance (now public), embarrassing as it is, because I am certain it is an important factor in my approach.

The Story Behind - Too Much Punch For Judy by Mark Wheeller

Diary

19 January 1987

I wonder if this Too Much Punch production will merely be an appendix to Quenchers or lead to something that stands on its own two feet?

The quality of today's and yesterday's rehearsal and pleasingly, my own invention, means this could become my most mature and best production to date.

Five of the original cast from Edinburgh remain: John Rowley: now auditioning for Drama Schools and our oldest member - 20 - continues to play Duncan. Barrie Sapsford: our most loyal member, with 11 productions to his credit, now plays Chris Caten.

Fay Davies: intends to pursue an acting career and remains as Toni. Nick Fradd: commanded my respect on lights. Jodi: still the youngest in the group but not the least experienced, plays Phyllis to John R's Captain Assertive in what has now become the opening scene.

The new members are all drawn from the current 4th year (Year 10). Garth Jennings came on board tonight as a techie doing slides and sound.

I have entered the production for the National Student Drama Festival (NSDF). This Festival targets the post 16 age group but some schools do get in, notably John Godber's previous school, Minsthorpe High.

This offers us something special to aim for and an additional motivating factor for me. I will be astounded should we not qualify and once we get there, if we fail to run away with many of the awards. I am supremely confident.

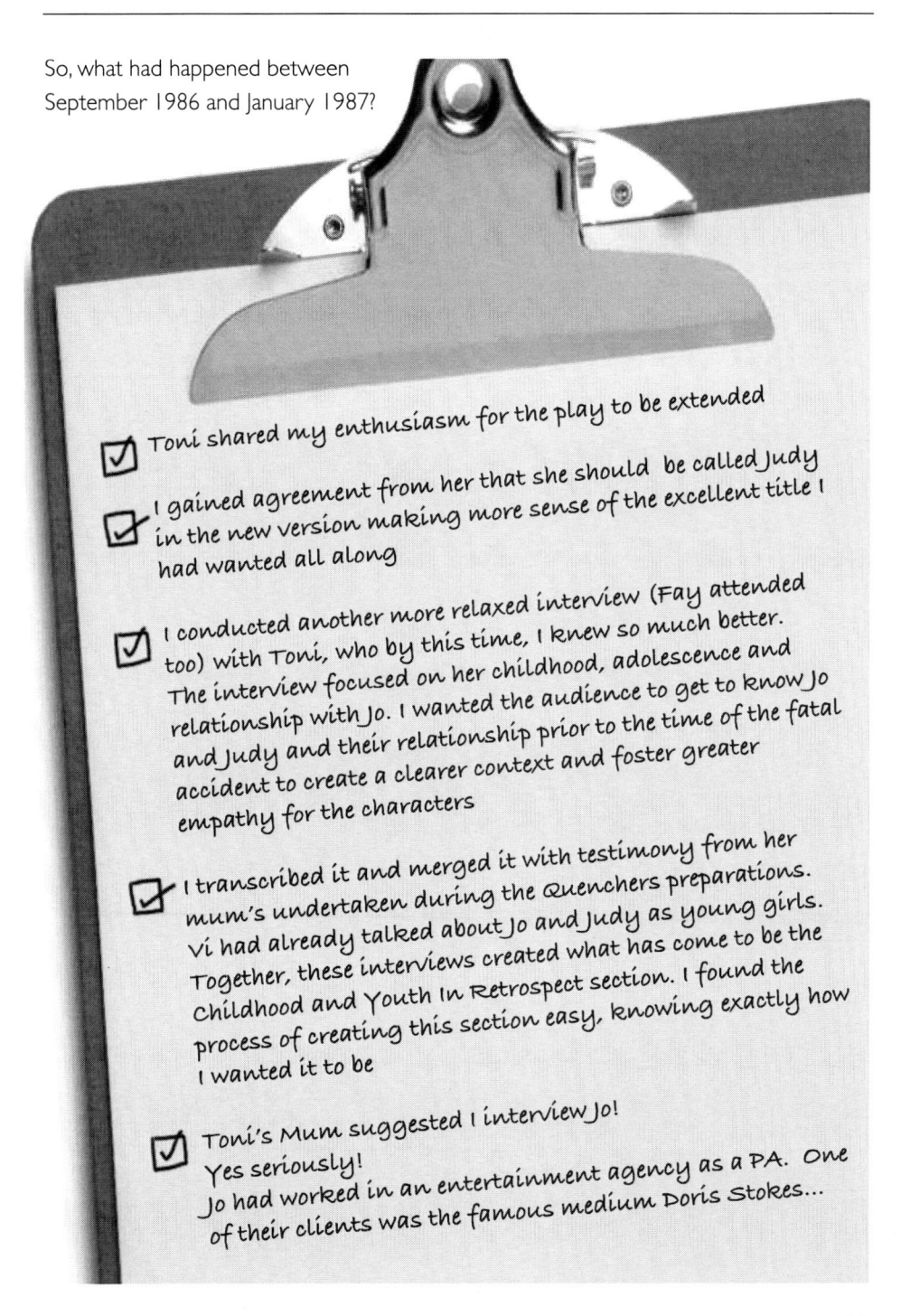

The Story Behind - Too Much Punch For Judy by Mark Wheeller

So, what had happened between September 1986 and January 1987?

- ☑ Toni shared my enthusiasm for the play to be extended

- ☑ I gained agreement from her that she should be called Judy in the new version making more sense of the excellent title I had wanted all along

- ☑ I conducted another more relaxed interview (Fay attended too) with Toni, who by this time, I knew so much better. The interview focused on her childhood, adolescence and relationship with Jo. I wanted the audience to get to know Jo and Judy and their relationship prior to the time of the fatal accident to create a clearer context and foster greater empathy for the characters

- ☑ I transcribed it and merged it with testimony from her mum's undertaken during the Quenchers preparations. Vi had already talked about Jo and Judy as young girls. Together, these interviews created what has come to be the Childhood and Youth In Retrospect section. I found the process of creating this section easy, knowing exactly how I wanted it to be

- ☑ Toni's Mum suggested I interview Jo! Yes seriously! Jo had worked in an entertainment agency as a PA. One of their clients was the famous medium Doris Stokes...

The Story Behind - Too Much Punch For Judy by Mark Wheeller

... Vi said she had spoken to Jo in a séance and had an interesting take on the accident. I did not ask what this was and did not accept the offer. I remember thinking (all too academically) whether this account would be "plausible to use in a documentary play". I also wondered how my mentor Roy Nevitt (and his before him, Peter Cheeseman) would have dealt with this request. My overriding feeling was that any account Jo might give me would devalue the authenticity of the play. I regret my decision. I would have been under no obligation to include anything that was "said" and it would have been fascinating to be part of such an "event" with a renowned medium such as Doris

I had to decide on how the play would open.

* I wanted it to be with a bang; particularly bearing in mind my ultimate aim for it to become a Theatre in Education piece.

* The Childhood and Youth In Retrospect section was wordy and not lively enough.

* I had two existing options: Captain Assertive or Happy Soap. Both provided a contrast with the drama of the main story. My innate laziness surfaced and I didn't consider writing anything new. I loved Happy Soap but felt it may play "too young".

* I settled on a barely altered Captain Assertive as the opening scene. I never at any stage thought Captain Assertive was the perfect opening scene but did not want to face the problem of what else to do. No one questioned me, so it happened. It was patently a "bolt on" and until about a week before the production I made little attempt to link it to the main story. It was there purely to offer a contrastingly lively opening and provide a theatrical hook

The Story Behind - Too Much Punch For Judy by Mark Wheeller

John Rowley as Captain Assertive and Jo Dumelow as Phyllis "flying" through the "sky"

I remember thinking **Happy Soap** might also have a future. I thought it could provide an opportunity for younger performers in a separate curtain raiser. **Too Much Punch** had a running time of about 45 minutes. I was concerned this wouldn't be value for money for an audience. I didn't have time to mount a separate **Happy Soap** production as well but have since seen schools use it as the first part of an evening's entertainment. (NB This is not the full length musical version, **Wacky Soap**, which might necessitate the audience camping overnight!).

Rehearsals started in October.

Half the play was already blocked (from **Quenchers**) so we were primarily concerned with developing a way of staging the new sections.

I was keen to make the play more physical as it didn't have the more lively **Quenchers** scenes to set it up.

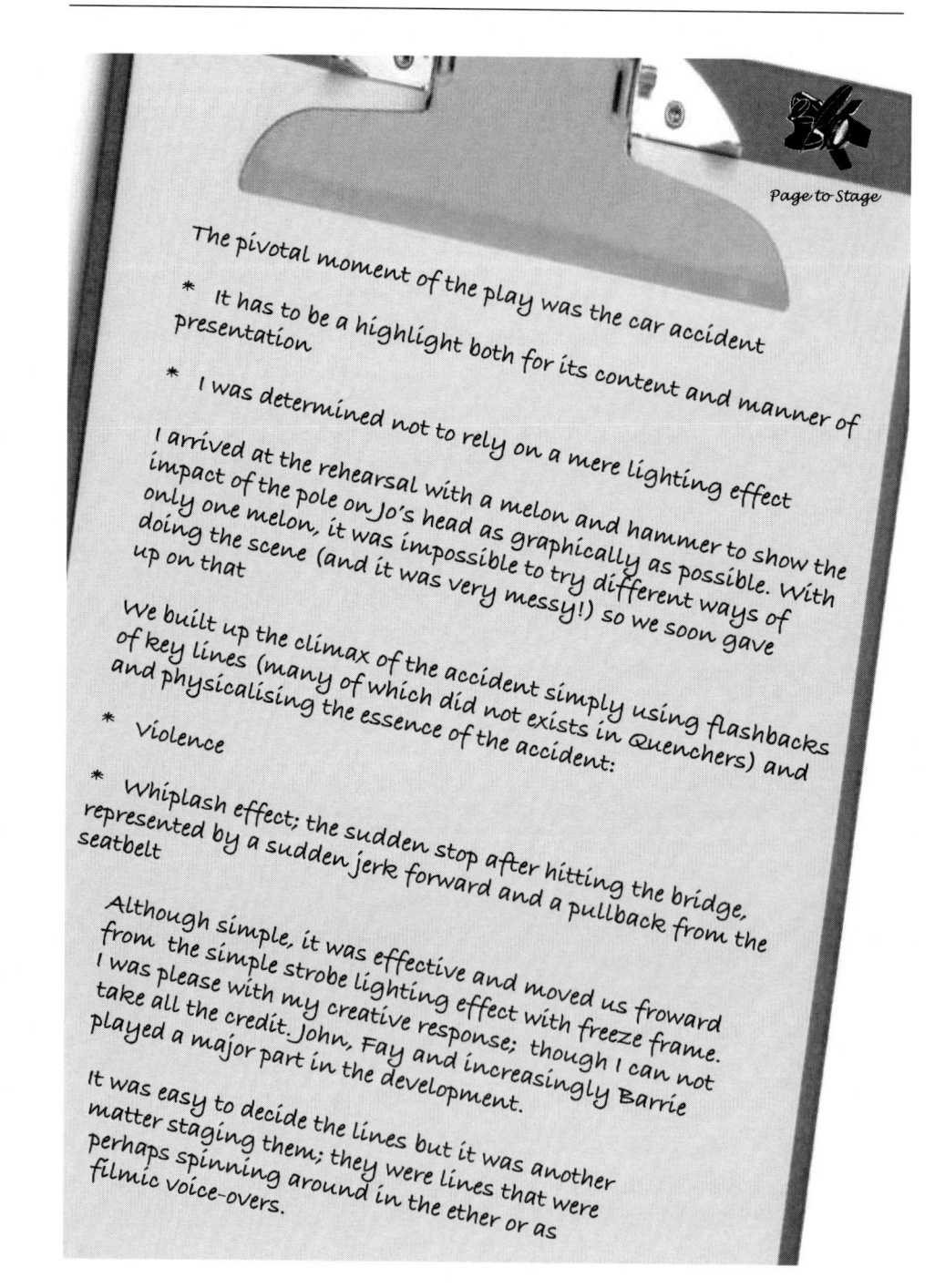

The Story Behind - Too Much Punch For Judy by Mark Wheeller

The pivotal moment of the play was the car accident

* It has to be a highlight both for its content and manner of presentation

* I was determined not to rely on a mere lighting effect

I arrived at the rehearsal with a melon and hammer to show the impact of the pole on Jo's head as graphically as possible. With only one melon, it was impossible to try different ways of doing the scene (and it was very messy!) so we soon gave up on that

We built up the climax of the accident simply using flashbacks of key lines (many of which did not exists in Quenchers) and physicalising the essence of the accident:

* Violence

* Whiplash effect; the sudden stop after hitting the bridge, represented by a sudden jerk forward and a pullback from the seatbelt

Although simple, it was effective and moved us froward from the simple strobe lighting effect with freeze frame. I was please with my creative response; though I can not take all the credit. John, Fay and increasingly Barrie played a major part in the development.

It was easy to decide the lines but it was another matter staging them; they were lines that were perhaps spinning around in the ether or as filmic voice-overs.

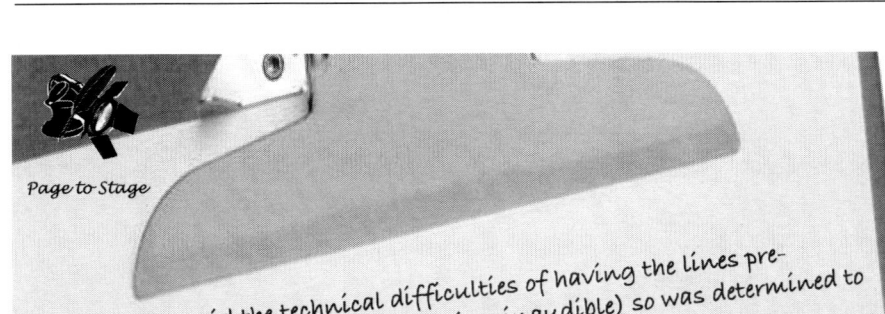

The Story Behind - Too Much Punch For Judy by Mark Wheeller

Page to Stage

I wanted to avoid the technical difficulties of having the lines pre-recorded (and therefore risk them being inaudible) so was determined to have them said on stage.

This forced us to look at the scene from a non-naturalistic point of view, which bought about a more theatrical approach to the scene.

We were all excited by the freshness of what we were doing. We had no templates from productions we had seen and stepped into the dark to invent.

The success of staging this scene lead me to consider imaginative ways to stage the moment where, in the real situation, Vi passed out when she heard that Jo had been killed. It had seemed too melodramatic in the original production, so we simply ignored what we knew had happened. We were well aware that Vi falling to the floor must not make the audience laugh.

I imagined what might cause Vi to faint as she is being given this "every mothers nightmare" news.

Her head must have been swirling with thoughts.

I asked two people to go on stage, unseen by Chris and Vi (as they perform their naturalistic scene)

I wondered if the two additional performers might interact with Vi and perhaps help place her on the floor and suggested they superimpose words into the ongoing revelation scene; Duncan's angry account of the "bloody woman driving the bloody car who couldn't have touched the brakes" speech together with lines recounting the final meeting of Vi and Jo.

The cast "played" with my incomplete and fragmented ideas. The resultant scene became stylised and not laughter inducing.

Interestingly it became more "real" though far less naturalistic!

The Story Behind - Too Much Punch For Judy by Mark Wheeller

By January rehearsals were progressing well and plans surrounding the future of the play were continuing apace!

The IAS, who provided us with the *Quenchers* drink, had, unbeknown to us, sent Judy Cornwall (actress, best known for her role as Daisy in *Keeping Up Appearances*) to review our Edinburgh performance.

> *"I was so impressed by the techniques used to give information about the dangers of alcohol abuse that at the end of the review I said: I would like to see Quenchers published and made available to schools all over the country."*

I convinced them to wait and publish *Too Much Punch For Judy* instead!

They wanted to release it no later than the start of the following school year (September 1987) on a limited run of 3,000 copies.

It was a massive affirmation of my work before it had even been performed!

I agreed to provide them with a "final copy" after the performances when changes would be implemented with the benefit of seeing it on stage with audience reactions.

Releasing a script means control over productions goes out of my hands. I know I was fearful that overacting in a melodramatic style would ruin this play. To try and counteract this I wrote a paragraph for the introduction to the play script. I still ensure this paragraph appears in the introduction to all my documentary plays. What I can't control is how many read it! It is, in my view, a key to the success of staging these plays.

> "It must at all times be remembered when reading or performing this play that the events it portrays are as close to the truth as memory and honesty allow. The performers should not impersonate the real-life characters (it is unlikely that they will know them to be able to do so) but breathe into them a life that is a reasonable interpretation of the words in the script. Unless specifically instructed to do otherwise for a particular effect, the actors should avoid overstatement and veer towards underplaying. Trust the material. It is after all as near as possible a realistic account of events."

The Story Behind - Too Much Punch For Judy by Mark Wheeller

I think Brecht (whose theories I hadn't read at that time) clearly had a major part to play in this thinking. My approach had been developed from papers I'd read on documentary theatre by Peter Cheeseman and in my conversations with Roy Nevitt.

Quenchers had served the purpose of building interest towards what had now become the main event. Our job now was to ensure people would not be disappointed!

The week before the performances we took delivery of £400 worth of sound equipment for our Drama Studio. The previous term we had a fire door installed to enable us to use it as a public performance venue. The large school hall would have provided the wrong atmosphere for this play, which is why we had never done public performances of *Quenchers* at the school. The "Studio" was perfect. *Punch* became the first play to be performed in this intimate space! Five performances and a preview were planned for the second week of February.

As we started to run through the play we found we were struggling with the section where Judy is admitted to hospital.

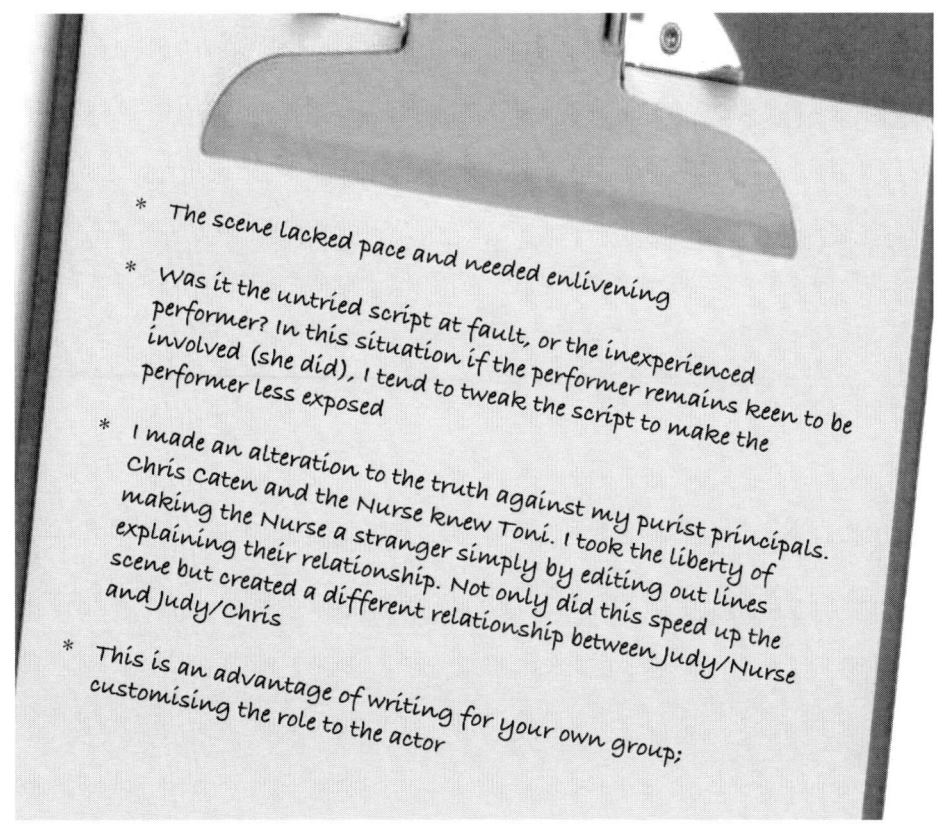

> * The scene lacked pace and needed enlivening
> * Was it the untried script at fault, or the inexperienced performer? In this situation if the performer remains keen to be involved (she did), I tend to tweak the script to make the performer less exposed
> * I made an alteration to the truth against my purist principals. Chris Caten and the Nurse knew Toni. I took the liberty of making the Nurse a stranger simply by editing out lines explaining their relationship. Not only did this speed up the scene but created a different relationship between Judy/Nurse and Judy/Chris
> * This is an advantage of writing for your own group; customising the role to the actor

The Story Behind - Too Much Punch For Judy by Mark Wheeller

The production was nearly upon us. John and I invented a link between Captain Assertive and the main story the week before the performance.

Captain Assertive stumbles across Jo and Judy as they leave the wine bar.

They ignore his warning and go on to have their fatal accident.

This wonderful line (not) will give you an idea of where we were:

Judy: Do you really think we'd listen to some comic strip character telling us not to drink? What do you know about the real world?

C. A.: Come on Phyllis. It seems we've outstayed our welcome. Let's leave before we're completely "torn apart" and leave the real world to deal with its own problems. Enjoy your evening!

We also added a little phrase at the end of that scene:

"Much is done in ignorance"

This was also repeated by the cast and directed towards Jo and Judy, one word at a time with the final word, "ignorance" spoken in unison (a technique I went on to use frequently to enliven or amplify lines) and with jazz hands! The over the top performance of this line contrasted with Jo and Judy's tragic tale.

I'm well aware that in the cold light of day this doesn't seem that impressive but believe me, I was relieved to justify the inclusion of the Captain Assertive scene and, if nothing else, kick off the play with a lively start!

It would be another year before the beginnings of the current opening scene would emerge (where "much is done in ignorance" remains, albeit without the jazz hands!).

Leading up to the first performances I was confident but still had anxious moments:

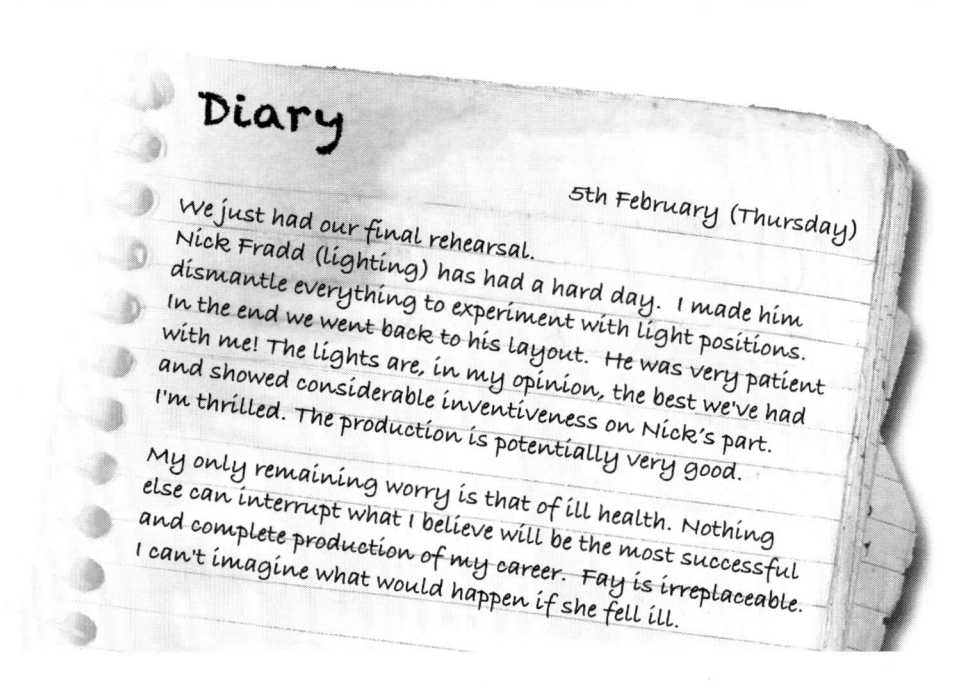

The Story Behind - Too Much Punch For Judy by Mark Wheeller

> **Diary** *5th February (Thursday)*
>
> We just had our final rehearsal. Nick Fradd (lighting) has had a hard day. I made him dismantle everything to experiment with light positions. In the end we went back to his layout. He was very patient with me! The lights are, in my opinion, the best we've had and showed considerable inventiveness on Nick's part. I'm thrilled. The production is potentially very good.
>
> My only remaining worry is that of ill health. Nothing else can interrupt what I believe will be the most successful and complete production of my career. Fay is irreplaceable. I can't imagine what would happen if she fell ill.

The new cast members were much younger than those they replaced in *Quenchers* and none had previously performed in public.

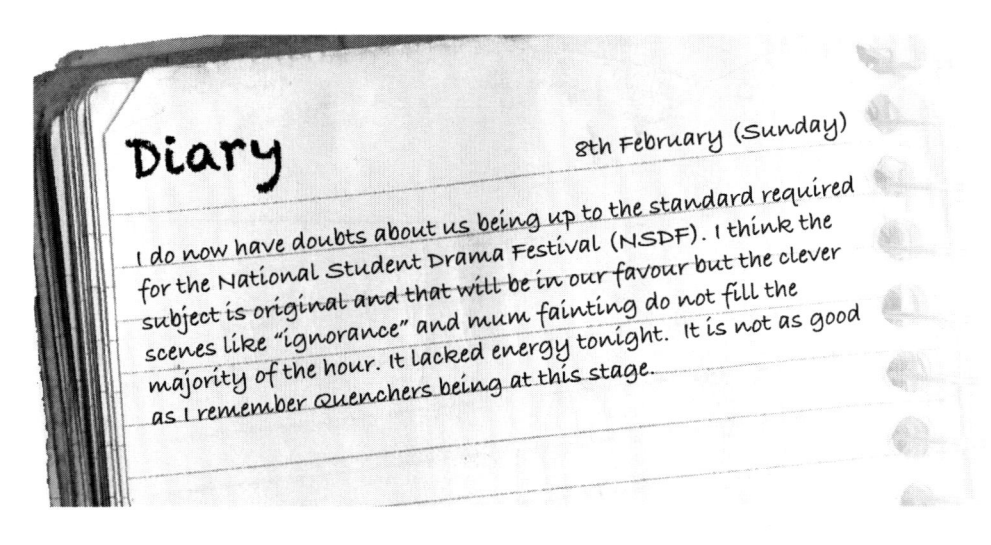

> **Diary** *8th February (Sunday)*
>
> I do now have doubts about us being up to the standard required for the National Student Drama Festival (NSDF). I think the subject is original and that will be in our favour but the clever scenes like "ignorance" and mum fainting do not fill the majority of the hour. It lacked energy tonight. It is not as good as I remember Quenchers being at this stage.

The Story Behind - Too Much Punch For Judy by Mark Wheeller

How short was my memory?

I was nervously looking forward to the following week when *Too Much Punch For Judy* would receive its first performances.

We were to be featured by ITV's brand-new TVAM with, not only extracts from the play but also, a live interview with Fay and Toni. I was disappointed not to be included in this (particularly as they were to be paid what I considered handsome expenses!) but was on the edge of my seat watching. It made a big impression on the program makers and was invaluable coverage for us.[21]

This little production in our tiny Drama Studio gained national coverage which none of our better known productions had achieved.

This flushed away the commonly held misapprehension that presenting well-known productions is the only way a Youth Theatre secures an audience for its work.

This level of coverage was an advantage I had never considered and it wasn't to be a one off.

My original productions garner more media interest than others.

Now all we needed was an invitation to perform at the NSDF. I remained optimistic!

---

[21] *This footage is now available to see on YouTube.*

The Story Behind - Too Much Punch For Judy by Mark Wheeller

7. Too Much Punch For Judy -
First Performance and the NSDF!

We were certainly reaching out to an audience beyond friends and parents!

On the 9th of February we did a preview performance to a selection of people.

I remember Andy Graham from *SNAP Theatre Company* attended at my invitation. Andy, who had directed Kes all those years before, was still working with SNAP and had come to know me as I often invited them to perform at our school. He asked me to join their board of directors, which I took as a massive compliment. In turn he gave his time to be supportive of our efforts.

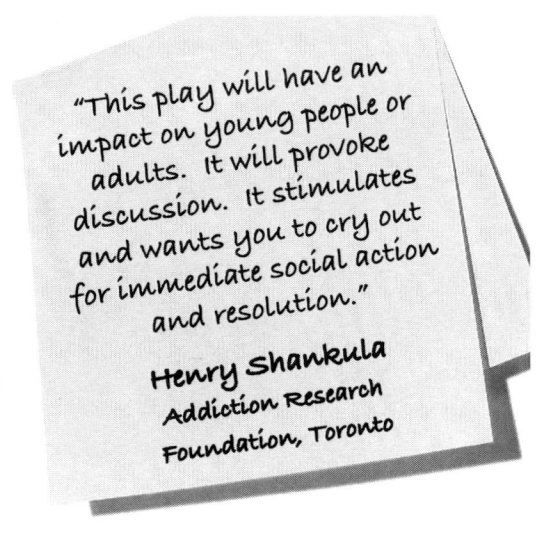

> "This play will have an impact on young people or adults. It will provoke discussion. It stimulates and wants you to cry out for immediate social action and resolution."
>
> Henry Shankula
> Addiction Research Foundation, Toronto

I remember being disappointed that he seemed nonplussed by our performance. To be fair, the only response I was looking for was simply:

"That is the best play I have ever seen. It was perfect! Can we tour it?"

I don't imagine he was at all discouraging but the fact he wasn't completely bowled over proved frustrating for me. Maybe it wasn't as good as I had imagined. The one sentence I recorded in my diary about the reaction from our visitors was:

> **Diary**
> We did a run through and received some useful criticisms.

I know we would have done what we could to address the issues raised by these "useful criticisms". No doubt we had a rehearsal and went through everything in detail making alterations where needed.

The Story Behind - Too Much Punch For Judy by Mark Wheeller

I had also invited **Touchstone**, who by now, it seemed, might be in the right place at the right time to mount a professional production fast. That said; no one was counting chickens just yet; certainly not before the public performances. I don't remember how they reacted to the performance that night, which would suggest they weren't bowled over either! However, Phil, one of the Touchstone team remembers differently:

> We remember the Youth Theatre production and how impactful it was. I admit I never had much of a taste for raw emotional stuff and don't forget I was a struggling writer and would have begrudged on principle someone else's work being successful! However, it was clear in performance how well it worked as a piece of theatre. I think any kid who saw it took the pledge there and then!

We presented five performances that week.

Reviewers from local papers and the Times Educational Supplement attended. By chance they sent a new reviewer, Nick Baker. With the play lasting only 55 minutes I thought even Hugh David might have stayed to see the whole thing! In any case the layout of the room would make it difficult for anyone to leave early, as to exit they would have to walk across the stage.

My diary records the following reactions to these performances and the all-important (to me) *NSDF* adjudication:

Diary

12th February 1987 (Thursday)

The performance was great! Fay was incredible. People were crying and everyone I spoke to thought it was better than Quenchers.

I experienced a sense of anti-climax afterwards. The ending is a downer, so the audience reaction is somewhat muted. Had it ended on Captain Assertive things might be different. Last night's audience were almost exclusively 4th and 5th years. They were incredibly attentive, proving it does work as a Theatre in Education piece

The Story Behind - Too Much Punch For Judy by Mark Wheeller

Toni had also come to see it:

> *"It was better than Quenchers. It had more effect. It's not something I can enjoy. I switch off emotionally, otherwise I'd cry. When you're not ready for it, it gives you a bit of a wallop. I feel sorry for those who are upset by it and then I realise they're probably feeling sorry for me!"*

The most incredible reaction came from my downstairs neighbour. He'd lived in the flat below me for a few years. He knew what my job was but we had never talked about what I did in detail. He was a mechanic and my main contact with him over the years was asking him questions about my unreliable cars! He had heard about *Too Much Punch* from the media coverage particularly in the Epping Gazette, which seemed to feature us most weeks! I was surprised that he was interested but secured complementary tickets for him to thank him for all his advice.

At the end of the production he approached me and was really choked. He was gobsmacked by the production but what had hit him the hardest was that as soon as the slides of Jo and "Judy" were shown he realised he knew them both from school. Jo had been in his class. He had no idea she had been killed: He was devastated. It was not the evening he was anticipating. I didn't quite know what to say but it did serve to re-enforce the whole reality of this incident for me.

The first printed review came from the Theatre reviewer for the West Essex Gazette (as opposed to a local reporter, who we were lucky enough to have as well). The second was from a reporter from Ongar, where Jo and Toni had been brought up. I was in for a shock!

REVIEWS

The Drinking Menace

The knowledge it was based on fact made it all the poignant... The play keeps hammering the message home without restraint. It made an impact but could have made just as much impression without the constant repetition and overuse of foul language, which was not a good idea for these very young children who may think that should be the way they must express themselves.

Phyl Romeril

The Story Behind - Too Much Punch For Judy by Mark Wheeller

> **Ongar and Brentwood Gazette: Arts news. Vital message.**
>
> ***Too Much Punch For Judy*** is a startlingly effective documentary performed by the highly talented members of EYT. Fay Davis played Judy with complete authority, though with little fancy diction and conveyed perfectly the anguish and despair at the consequences of her action. Beth Spendlow matched her with a fine performance as the doomed Joanna while Debbie Mitchell gave an astonishingly mature account in the role of the mother.
>
> The script has an earthy quality that is entirely plausible, although a personal belief holds that the obscenities and blasphemies demeaned the chief characters without adding anything to the drama.
> ***John Hutton***

As usual, I focussed on the negative in both reviews (I've only shown extracts here), the criticism of the bad language. Toni used the "f" word without inhibition in the interviews and I had included it where she had said it in the script to retain authenticity. Around this time popular music TV program, The Tube was taken off air because someone used the "f" word before the watershed. I did not want the school or myself to get into trouble.

I called a meeting of the cast half an hour before that evenings performance saying we were in danger of the message in the play being hijacked! If these reviewers were offended, other people could be too. There was a brief discussion but the cast agreed.

The Story Behind - Too Much Punch For Judy by Mark Wheeller

* We only had these five performances to make our mark

* The TES were reviewing it that night. We did not want this discussion to go national

* The performance went ahead without the "f" word bar one, at the moment where Judy pushes Duncan away shouting "Don't fucking touch me!" Fay tells me I was insistent that this should stay, although in the first edition of the script it became "bloody"… and I had to fight for that!

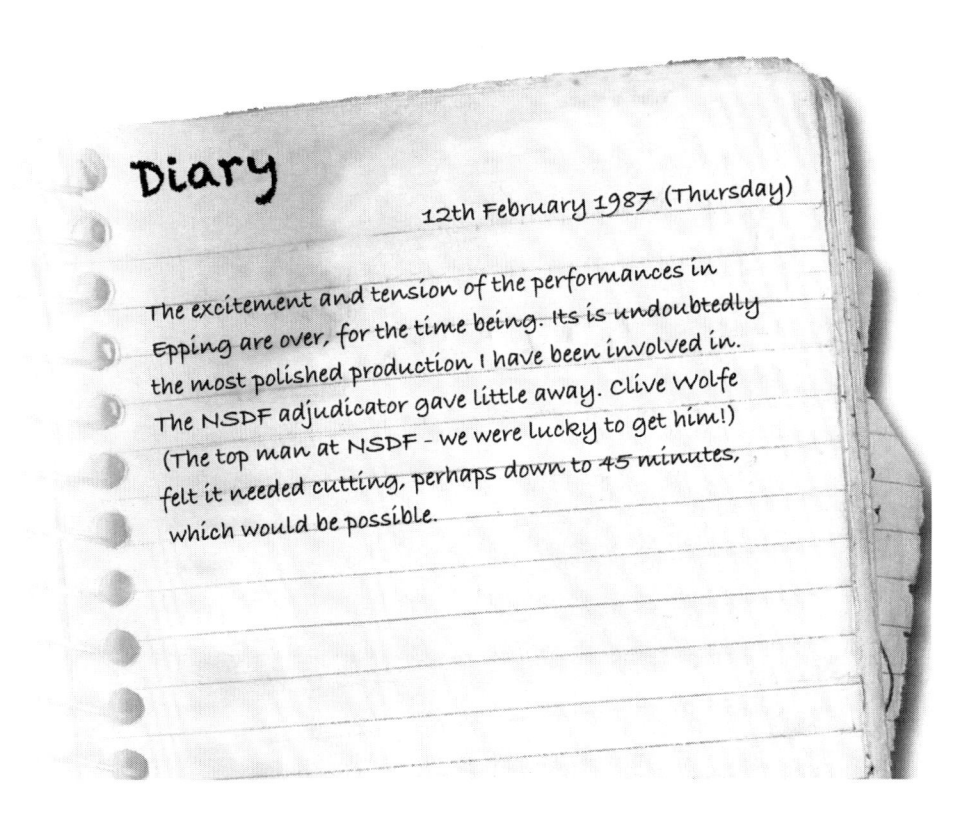

Diary

12th February 1987 (Thursday)

The excitement and tension of the performances in Epping are over, for the time being. Its is undoubtedly the most polished production I have been involved in. The NSDF adjudicator gave little away. Clive Wolfe (The top man at NSDF - we were lucky to get him!) felt it needed cutting, perhaps down to 45 minutes, which would be possible.

The Story Behind - Too Much Punch For Judy by Mark Wheeller

We had to wait another week for more reviews to be published. However, the audience reaction was superb.

Nevertheless, I spent that week improving the script for our performance at the IAS. The cast were, as ever, willing to implement the changes I made so we could present the "final" amended script.

Diary

21st February 1987

I have added two bits from my final interview with Toni. The first is the addition of the Tarot card scene, which is significant and, because of the way she expresses her fears, which are amusing. I have also added a new spine tingling ending where she says, "If I had one wish" etc. That should make a lot of difference.

We did a goodish performance at the Institute of Alcohol Studies. The more I think about it, the less impressed I am, but those attending the conference were bowled over. I'm proud to be associated with it and want it to be my finale in Epping. I have itchy feet.

The Story Behind - Too Much Punch For Judy by Mark Wheeller

When the reviews came out they were all we could hope for!

REVIEWS

West Essex Gazette: This Punch Pulled no Punches

A statistic of death come alive… (it) leaves nerves raw and twanging. The secret lies in one word: reality. The outstanding performance of the evening came from Barrie Sapsford as PC Chris Caten, facing a double-dilemma as the family's personal friend and police officer to break the news of Joanna's death. The relationship of the two sisters, only touched on, is a familiar incongruity - the bright, beautiful, promising sister dies while Judy, living in her shadow and resentful of it, survives. This play ought to make much more than a dent in public consciousness.

Alison Burnett

REVIEW

Epping Star: Drink Drive Drama.

Everyone who's ever been tempted to drink and drive should see **Too Much Punch For Judy**… the horrors of the true-life fatal accident and the emotional effects the tragedy has on the people concerned… a personal success for each of the young actors, who performed like professionals, touching every emotion of the audience.

"EME"

The Story Behind - Too Much Punch For Judy by Mark Wheeller

REVIEWS

Amateur Stage

A sparkling production that began by grabbing its studio audience by the throat and then with an abrupt change of mood and style, immersed us in a tragedy… a real tragedy too… Mark Wheeller used the words of the people involved as the dialogue for his young actors… the result is a poignant story about avoidable casual death. What most lingers is the sincerity and vigour of these skilful young actors. Fay Davis as Judy was particularly impressive, closely matched by that of John Rowley as the first person present at the crash. It was a local tragedy, but, it could have happened anywhere, to any family you know.

"C.H"

The big review (in my opinion at least) was the TES:

TES REVIEW

Times Educational Supplement: Punch Drunk
Too Much Punch For Judy Epping Youth Theatre

The young players performed with steely concentration and a minimum of sentimentality. The equally young audience I sat in was patently out for some whooping Friday night fun watching their mates on stage. At the end, there was a horrid silence. Apart from a rather odd sequence at the beginning, in which Captain Assertive and his assistant Phyllis celebrate Superman style assertiveness, (the power to say no to that extra drink) Too Much Punch relentlessly ploughs one straight furrow. It's a piece of white propaganda, no more, no less. As theatre, it's one-dimensional. As part of the process of drama as educator it's a huge success.

Nick Baker

The Story Behind - Too Much Punch For Judy by Mark Wheeller

I still wonder what Hugh David would have made of it… and if he could have found a way to exit early.

The Essex County Council Highways Department were now committed to the professional tour and finalising arrangements with *Touchstone*. We investigated the possibility of EYT getting time off school but the logistics proved too difficult. A professional tour was the second best option, which we took as a massive compliment and I left them to it, as I was busy fielding calls from Clive Wolfe. I was getting carried away with myself, convinced we would be invited to perform at the *NSDF*… so much so that I organised an American buffet at my house on the afternoon the news as to which groups had been selected was to be divulged. I stipulated that we shouldn't start to eat until we knew the result.

> **Diary** — Sunday, 8 March
>
> 5:28 PM. Any minute now my house will be invaded by the Too Much Punch cast to find out whether or not we are one of the lucky 16 groups to be selected to participate in the 1988 NSDF. It will, I expect, be the devils own job to get through and I hope we don't make contact too soon, thus, the tension can build! I dare not get too confident for the fear of being let down. Statistically we only have a one in ten chance of being invited to perform.

In the event we got through fast. It was not the result I was hoping for.

> 8:08 in the evening:
> I'm afraid the NSDF turned us down, but we were shortlisted. We were in the final 21 (of about 150), which is an achievement. How have I reacted? Bitterly disappointed. I feel empty and lonely, as though someone important to me has walked out, or been taken from me. It leaves my year with a hole in it. Other than in publishing, I have not yet made my mark nationally. If I ever do get to the NSDF, it will make that achievement seem even greater. This, like getting a Fringe First, has become something I really want to achieve!
> The sad thing is that these performances may now merely become an appendix to the "big" Edinburgh ones. We were close. Close is not good enough…

The Story Behind - Too Much Punch For Judy by Mark Wheeller

> ... If we enter again with another production we stand no more chance. I don't think it is something where practice makes perfect, or experience improves. I cannot imagine I will ever be involved in anything as good as this again.

The atmosphere in my flat is a great example of anti-climax. I should have learnt from an experience back at school in the fourth year when, leaving a Maths exam I boasted to everyone how easy it had been. My confidence was misplaced and I failed the exam. My friends who had not shouted their views from the rooftops passed and laughed at me.

Perhaps it is that sense of optimism that allows me to continue to put myself forward in these competitive events.

> **Diary**   12th of March 1987
>
> Fay received a letter from Clive Wolfe praising her performance and inviting her to audition for the National Student Theatre Company. Well-done Fay, a well deserved plaudit.
> The Too Much Punch tour is in jeopardy with only nine bookings.

The Highways Department reacted strongly to the play not booking. They are determined to make it work. They ploughed a further £7000 into the tour enabling it to visit Essex schools for free. Schools took the bait.

Not only that but the Scottish Road Safety department booked a ten-week (two performances a day) tour to start in September 1987.

The Story Behind - Too Much Punch For Judy by Mark Wheeller

Too Much Punch For Judy was taking off!

Stan Dixon, our Head teacher at St. John's was sufficiently impressed that he suspended the timetable for all 3rd, 4th, 5th and 6th years (Year 9-13) to enable them to see us perform the play in school time in our little studio theatre. We did this over three days in a marathon of performances that Equity rules would never allow professional actors to do. My young cast loved it and, in that time we developed a wonderful sense of "togetherness". It made a deep impression on cast and audiences alike.

It also served to raise EYT's status in the school significantly. Most teachers hadn't seen our productions and they also saw cast members, and me, in a completely different, often more positive light.

We were invited to do our final performance by a friend of *Touchstone* in the fabulous Wyvern Theatre in Swindon. It gave us a sense of a "final performance" and provided a climax to our work:

> **Diary**
>
> 11th of April 1987
>
> Yesterday marked the final day of EYT's association with TMP. There was no sense of finality as we said our goodbyes in the Drama Studio at 1 o'clock in the morning! There was no feeling of emptiness when I returned to my house, but a feeling of great satisfaction.
>
> We returned from the best performance to an audience of about 40, who truly appreciated it. The big change was John's light-hearted approach to Duncan's lines, achieving a better contrast between the light and dark lines. Fay also found some humour in her "Spaghetti Bolognese" speech, which she did superbly.

The Story Behind - Too Much Punch For Judy by Mark Wheeller

We had tried, in our final rehearsals to find much needed lighter moments in the play.

Page to Stage

I asked John to perform Duncan's speeches altering every reference to the car accident to someone who had dropped some litter.

Although it seemed disrespectful it kept the speech alive and helped him develop new ideas to use in the performance. It was hilarious to watch as we all knew the seriousness of the real context.

John applied the "lift" to the speech when he presented it in that final performance.

This also demonstrates how we continued to "play" with the performance right through until the very end. We never thought, "We've sorted this".

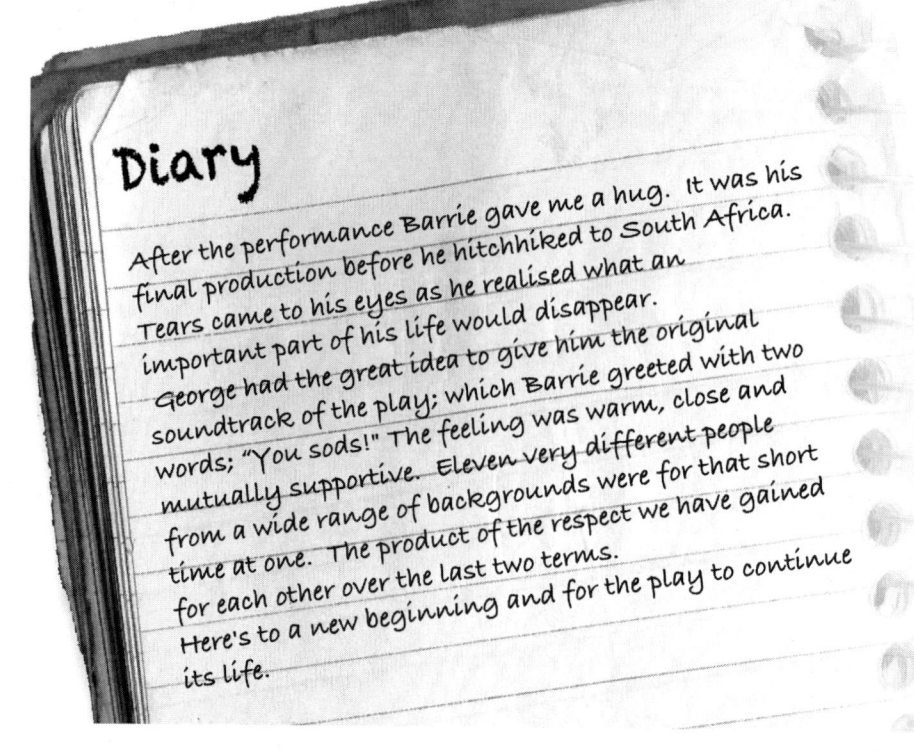

Diary

After the performance Barrie gave me a hug. It was his final production before he hitchhiked to South Africa. Tears came to his eyes as he realised what an important part of his life would disappear. George had the great idea to give him the original soundtrack of the play; which Barrie greeted with two words; "You sods!" The feeling was warm, close and mutually supportive. Eleven very different people from a wide range of backgrounds were for that short time at one. The product of the respect we have gained for each other over the last two terms. Here's to a new beginning and for the play to continue its life.

The Story Behind - Too Much Punch For Judy by Mark Wheeller

By then I had applied for a job in Southampton, at Oaklands Community School. This offered a huge promotion (financially and status) and an opportunity to develop a new Youth Theatre.

Within a month I was appointed to what, in my diary, I described as my "dream job".

The school was a new build (1982), with a progressive philosophy, in an area the newspapers had described as the Toxteth of Southampton! The Head, Peter Hollis, from Countesthorpe College in Leicestershire, famous for its progressive ideals, wanted to set up an "interesting", forward looking school. My background at Stantonbury helped me to land the job.

I was excited but somewhat scared by the prospect of starting again. It would provide me with a fresh challenge. I was not the only one to be moving on.

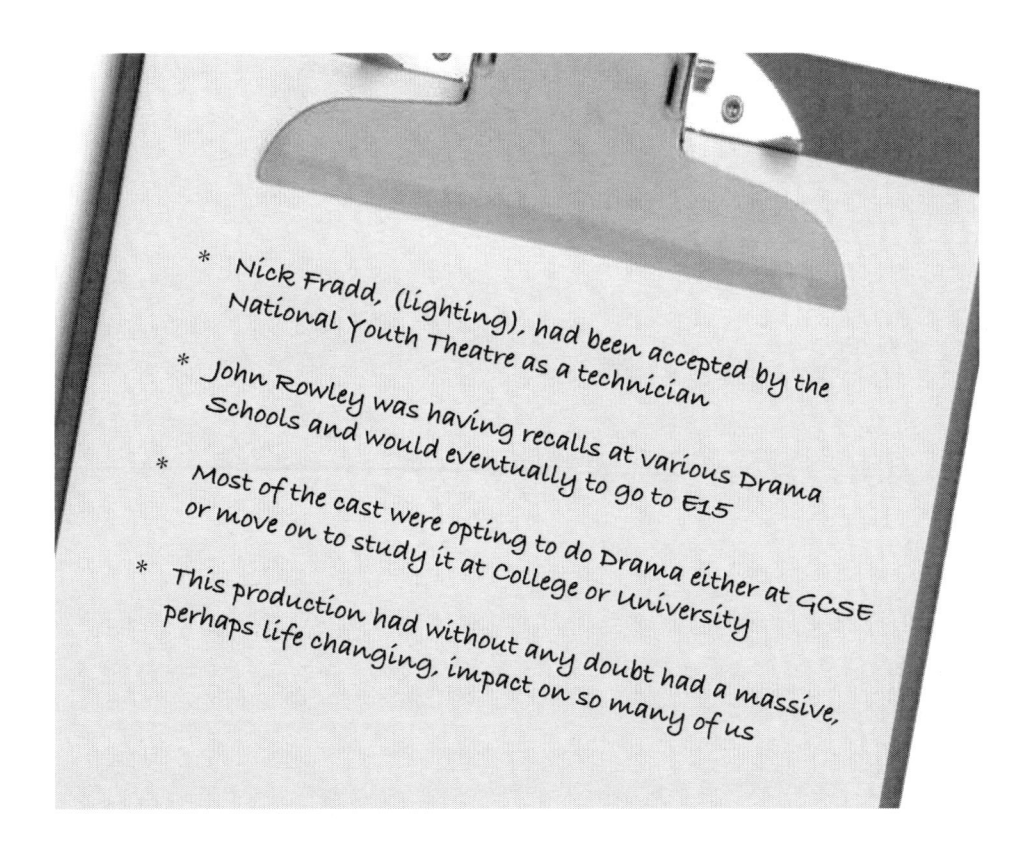

* Nick Fradd, (lighting), had been accepted by the National Youth Theatre as a technician
* John Rowley was having recalls at various Drama Schools and would eventually to go to E15
* Most of the cast were opting to do Drama either at GCSE or move on to study it at College or University
* This production had without any doubt had a massive, perhaps life changing, impact on so many of us

The Story Behind - Too Much Punch For Judy by Mark Wheeller

Now the play itself was to start out on its travels and make its impact in the world beyond Epping!

I remember when I left Epping I found the goodbyes difficult, particularly saying goodbye to EYT members. On my final night in Epping, the Youth Theatre and I went out for a meal. I cried for the first time in years.

I was excited by the opportunities that awaited me in Southampton but was all too aware of what I was leaving behind.

Epping Youth Theatre had grown from nothing to something very special. We had produced original work, which was now to be taken on further by professionals.

Our efforts over the last three years had also fully equipped the little Drama classroom to become a fully-fledged Drama Studio and public performance space.

> EYT stopped very soon after you left. In any case it wasn't the same. It didn't work. That was hard for me. A lot of things happened all at once; you leaving, the end of EYT, loss of all those other friends who left at the same time. I remember you coming down with the kids from your new school & feeling extremely jealous!
> **Jodi - 2011**

I remember that too.

It happened at a time when I was seriously questioning whether I had made the right decision to move. Jodi was performing her self-devised piece for her final GCSE exam two years after I'd left Epping. I took some of my fourth year students from Oaklands who needed to see a model of outstanding work to inspire them. My year 11's at that time, at Oaklands were not able to offer that (understatement).

Jodi had led her GCSE group in devising a play called *"What Do Monsters Really Look Like?"* Their story used famous children's rhymes as their text, culminating with the question (of the title) being answered by a slide of Myra Hindley projected onto a sheet at the back of the stage.

It was such an imaginative and daring piece for a group of sixteen year olds to create. She would not have been capable of this without the *Too Much Punch* experience.

The evening showed my Oaklands group what it was possible to achieve and left me feeling I had not made the right decision to move. I wondered how long it would take to achieve that standard of work in Southampton. Indeed could my Oaklands students ever go on to reach the imaginative heights Jodi and her group had achieved, seemingly without effort.

The Story Behind - Too Much Punch For Judy by Mark Wheeller

My students were inspired by that evening's performances and went on to produce incredible work themselves the following year.

One sub-group in that class presented a documentary of the Hillsborough Disaster, which still ranks as one of the best devised GCSE pieces I have ever seen.

That evening in Epping provided a crucial stepping-stone in the journey to a new level of Drama presentation at Oaklands from which we never looked back. The *Too Much Punch* snowball continues to this day for my students and myself.

John Rowley's 1986 design for the first ***Too Much Punch For Judy*** book cover and subsequently the first professional school tour of the play.

The Story Behind - Too Much Punch For Judy by Mark Wheeller

8. Too Much Punch For Judy - Enter the Professionals!

Touchstone had worked in St John's for nearly a year as a resident Theatre Company and they had been fun to work with. They developed their own projects independently and collaborated on others with me. They directed EYT in a production of Alan Ayckbourn's *Absurd Person Singular* which Fay (Judy) remembers being a "happy experience".

I devised a fantastic project with them called *Cultures*, which I describe at length in my *Drama Schemes* book. (22)

"If we can let go and trust things will work out the way they're supposed to, without trying to control the outcome, then we can begin to enjoy the moment more fully. The joy of the freedom it brings becomes more pleasurable than the experience itself."
Goldie Hawn

This was a life rate, spontaneous role-play session with three classes in the third year (Year 9) in three rooms simultaneously. At the end of the day all 80+ students come together for a climatic spontaneous in role encounter.

Touchstone was, as far as I was concerned, Helen and Phil. They were my only points of contact.

Unbeknown to me, until I came to research this book, Helen and a friend of hers, Rose, were the co-directors. Phil was Helen's partner and an actor/writer, merely working for Touchstone. I was well aware that, like myself, they were not from the same mould as the people portrayed in the *Too Much Punch* story. I assumed they would have also been aware of these differences so imagined they would deal with this when they cast the play.

It shocked me when they told me Helen was to play Judy.

I had also anticipated Phil would direct. I was entirely happy with this. He had seen our production and knew how it had been.

They appointed a friend of theirs, a well thought of, up and coming director having worked at the *Royal Shakespeare Company* and the *Royal Opera House*. This seemed impressive but I had a nagging doubt. He had not seen our version of the play.

I tried to be positive and hoped this may prove advantageous. He could bring something exciting and new to the table.

(22) Published by Rhinegold 2009

The Story Behind - Too Much Punch For Judy by Mark Wheeller

A meeting was arranged between the newly appointed director, David and myself.

I remember approaching this meeting feeling overawed by him with his lofty credentials

I assumed when we met he would be sensitive to this and put me at my ease.

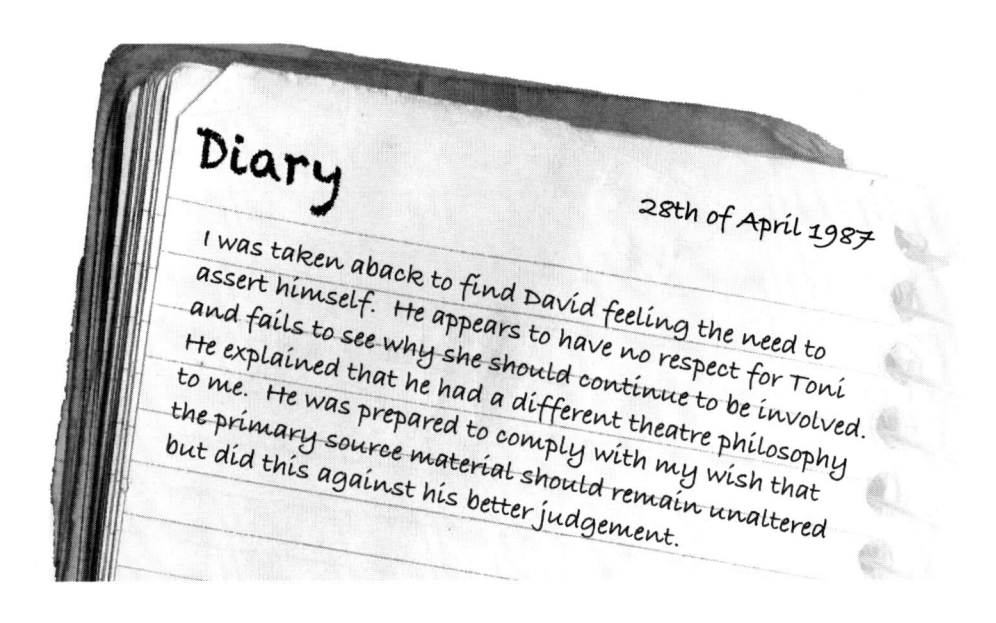

> **Diary**
> *28th of April 1987*
>
> I was taken aback to find David feeling the need to assert himself. He appears to have no respect for Toni and fails to see why she should continue to be involved. He explained that he had a different theatre philosophy to me. He was prepared to comply with my wish that the primary source material should remain unaltered but did this against his better judgement.

Why had he agreed to the direct the play?

He simply did not "get it"!

Alarm bells rang.

It was made all the more awkward because of my excellent relationship with Helen & Phil.

I began to regret allowing the professional production going out of my hands so easily.

I was out of my depth in these discussions but there was no time to backtrack.

The Story Behind - Too Much Punch For Judy by Mark Wheeller

Diary

28th of April 1987

David's worries about Toni interfering are unfounded. I tried, as best as I could to allay his fears. He showed me the accident scene, which he (or Touchstone) had adapted. I had to admit, it was better than ours. He (or Phil?) had played around imaginatively with the chronology so that the policeman's account cut into Judy's monologue. Sister Davies became Charge Nurse Davies due to casting issues. I had no problems with either but remember being frustrated that I was being told rather than involved in the process. Teasingly he would show me no more of the script, which, naively, I dared not question. I have the impression that other changes will be made. I am uncomfortable that this bears my name, but may actually not be my work. I am worried the rewrite will be better than my original! I was relieved to have been forthright about the primary source material otherwise all but the skeleton of the play might have been removed. When I spoke to Helen she asked nonchalantly:

"How did you get on? He's great isn't he?"

"Yes." I replied unable to come to terms fully with what had just happened.

He ripped into Judy's "guilt complex" and how this affects the "character". He kept referring to her as a "character". Toni being a real person was an inconvenience to him. He seemed to think I was blocking his 'artistic' endeavours. I fear they plan to portray Toni more unsympathetically than we did. He refuses to meet her, arguing that it would detrimentally affect their opportunities of being able to "interpret her character".

The Story Behind - Too Much Punch For Judy by Mark Wheeller

> *Having said all of this I state clearly; I remain confident about his directorial ability and hope he will make a real firecracker of the play.*
> *I cannot wait to see it!*

My reservations were allayed and my confidence borne out by the production, which I saw (with Toni!), on the 20th May 1987. I had no idea of the significance of this date, until I heard Helen, as Judy, say this line:

"The accident happened on the 20th May 1983."

A shiver went down my spine; I couldn't help but turn towards Toni. It emphasised even more forcefully that this was real.

> **Diary**
> *Too Much Punch For Judy by Touchstone proved to be very good. The comedy opening was far better than ours, but the body of the play itself, while having some bits that were better, was, as a whole, not as powerful. The acting was, at times too melodramatic and lacked the raw edge of ours. I've now seen it a couple of times in schools. It makes a good impact.*

I asked Phil for his recollections of the early days of the touring:

> "This was one of the first productions Touchstone undertook and played a major part in building the company's reputation, so it maintains a special place in our affections. We have an enduring memory of touring Essex in a Citroen 2CV, with Nev, the fourth Touchstone actor eating Edam and lime pickle sandwiches in the back. Meeting Toni had a strong impact on Helen. It was unsettling to meet the person she had been portraying on stage, knowing exactly what she had been through."
> **Phil Lowe (Touchstone Actor)**

The Touchstone production brought into sharp focus how unhappy I continued to be with the Captain Assertive opening. They had, understandably, refused to use it and gone ahead and written their original opening scene. I had no idea how to improve on Captain Assertive. I did sit down and scribble some alterations, but I knew it needed rewriting, not just tinkering with.

The Story Behind - Too Much Punch For Judy by Mark Wheeller

Phil offered me his alternative beginning (The Alcohol Overture), which, regardless of its quality, I would have never included. I wanted to crack it myself[23] and also, more importantly, there was the issue of ownership. I would have to share royalties!

I had no idea I could earn money from my plays being performed but after it had toured Essex, I was offered a royalty, by Touchstone, for the Scotland tour. I remember I bought a wardrobe with the payment! 150 actors applied for the four jobs. Other County Council Road Safety departments began to consider the production. It was at this point I realised - "this might have legs!"

John Rowley said we'd "missed a trick"; he was right. Neither of us had the experience nor time to do the legal stuff a company would require; audition actors, organise a tour, sort bookings and rehearse the performance. Having just secured a new job meant giving up teaching was not a realistic proposition. In any case Touchstone were there and ready to go. *Too Much Punch* would never have taken off were they not there to pick it up instantly!

My "difficult" relationship with David (their director) did not improve. I remember thinking I was made to feel like the amateur alongside the professional. He introduced me to the prospective actors at the audition for the Scottish tour as the "drama teacher at the school" rather than the "writer of the play". This made me start to become aware of "branding", though I would not have called it that then. Without a programme or my name appearing on a poster, no one was aware of my involvement. I chose not to question any of this for fear of appearing too much like a diva! I knew, once the script was published, my name would appear.

I attended the final rehearsal by the Scotland cast but left disappointed by a "rushed and unemotional" run through. It seemed to have lost the raw energy of the original EYT production and had become a half-hearted copy of the original Touchstone one.

There was one thing I was certain of. Professionals did not seem able to match Fay's raw performance of Judy. I put that down, rightly or wrongly, to their "proper" Drama School training.

I never expressed my reservations, thinking that for the duration of it being a touring production, which I didn't imagine would be long, Touchstone would be the Theatre Company to tour it and, for better or for worse, I had allowed it out of my control.

Suddenly the situation changed.

In 1988 Frank Nunnelly, a Road Safety Officer who had seen the original EYT production, approached me wanting to book six weeks (60 more performances) for Hertfordshire in the Autumn of 1988

---

[23] *I was not happy with the Bob and Nob opening until I re-wrote it for the 25th anniversary production in 2012. Finally I managed it!*

The Story Behind - Too Much Punch For Judy by Mark Wheeller

I approached Phil and he said Touchstone were "moving into new areas" so would not be interested. Initially I was concerned as I would have to put some time and effort into finding a company to do it and may be unsuccessful. The only other Theatre Company I knew were SNAP and I wasn't sure they'd be interested. Even if they were, I would be in the same position of having no control over what goes out.

What should I do? How could I bring it back to be the kind of production I wanted it to be?

I thought about John Rowley but he was about to start at E15.

However, Matt Allen, who played Graham in *Race To Be Seen,* was about to complete his course at the Guilford School of Acting. I wondered if he might be prepared to form a company and take *Too Much Punch* on tour?

I could work with Matt... He'd be sympathetic to the documentary approach.
I phoned him... Things moved far fast!

When Mark arrived in Epping I was in the fifth form at school and he had asked me to help him set up a Youth Theatre. I told him this would never work in Epping. However, once we got it going not only did everyone want to be in it; lots of people came to see the shows. We had such a great time.

At GSA my special project was on Community Theatre. I explained how at EYT we found stories from our community, which that same community would be interested in watching - such a great starting point.
I knew the strength of Punch and used it as an example. I called Fay Davies from my parent's house in Epping and asked her to recite Judy's speeches over the phone while I wrote them out. I edited them into one monologue, to tell the complete story. For my final second year project to the GSA first year students, I performed that monologue.

I saw an advert in The Stage for the professional production of Punch and applied. I performed that monologue at the audition. I hit them hard with the emotion, Stanislavsky style. I was into naturalism while Mark preferred Brecht. We had spent many a happy evening together arguing about which was better. They loved it and asked me to come back.
"Great!" I thought.
Then they hit me with it
"Come back next year when you've finished Drama school"
I was stunned!
Next year? Next year?!! Next year wasn't any good to me; I want to start now!

The Story Behind - Too Much Punch For Judy by Mark Wheeller

> Towards the end of my third year Mark approached me saying Frank Nunnelly from Hertfordshire wanted to book a professional touring production. I had no idea of costs but printed up some Ape Theatre Company Ltd notepaper and cobbled together a budget with everything I could think of. I arrived at Frank's office full of confidence but no idea of what I was doing.
> "Yes" I lied to Frank happily, "we've already produced lots of plays"
> I knew he wasn't buying into it but he didn't let on; well, not until later when we'd become friends. The meeting went well and Frank said he might book the show.
> "Might book it?" I said, "Hmm, what would swing it to WILL book it?"
> "Get Fay Davies to play Judy and you have a deal."
> Fay was 18 years old and about to leave college.
> I had to move fast.
> She had raw talent oozing out of her.
> I called her that evening and the deal was done.
> **Matt Allen (Ape Theatre Company)**

Ape hired me to direct the production.

I was back at the helm with 50% of the cast (Matt & Fay) ex Epping Youth Theatre members. The other two were friends of Matt's who had graduated from GSA. I didn't meet them until the first day of rehearsals. I trusted Matt's judgement.

For the rehearsal week we all shared a house in Guildford. This was organised by Matt (or probably his mum, Yvonne, as she is behind everything that needs organising with Ape).

Fay and her mum arrived shortly after I did. We hadn't seen each other for a year and had much to say. She had completed her college course and I had survived (just) my first year in a new school (always a wake up call)!

Our conversation was cut short when her mum called us from what was to be Fay's bedroom. Her mother had discovered the previous occupant had left a little gift; a used(?) durex in the bed. This gave us something to moan about when Matt arrived with Steve and Tor from GSA; not that Matt took our moans seriously!

I remember I planned to spend much of the first day of our weeklong rehearsals on a spontaneous improvisation.

My intention: to foster a natural acting approach and re-capture the raw energy of EYT.

I was also determined that the production would be openly emotional, something I felt Touchstone had achieved. We spent the whole of that first morning working off text and off subject on an improvisation I custom devised for this situation:

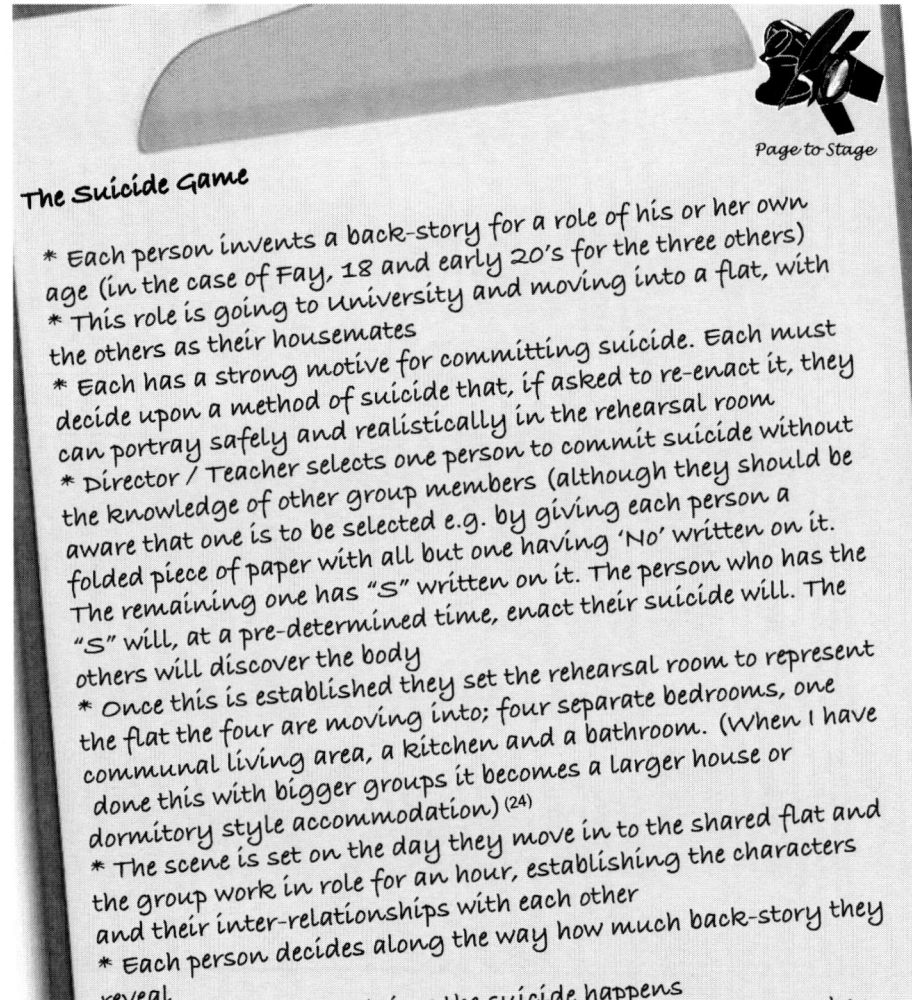

The Story Behind - Too Much Punch For Judy by Mark Wheeller

The Suicide Game

* Each person invents a back-story for a role of his or her own age (in the case of Fay, 18 and early 20's for the three others)
* This role is going to University and moving into a flat, with the others as their housemates
* Each has a strong motive for committing suicide. Each must decide upon a method of suicide that, if asked to re-enact it, they can portray safely and realistically in the rehearsal room
* Director / Teacher selects one person to commit suicide without the knowledge of other group members (although they should be aware that one is to be selected e.g. by giving each person a folded piece of paper with all but one having 'No' written on it. The remaining one has "S" written on it. The person who has the "S" will, at a pre-determined time, enact their suicide will. The others will discover the body
* Once this is established they set the rehearsal room to represent the flat the four are moving into; four separate bedrooms, one communal living area, a kitchen and a bathroom. (When I have done this with bigger groups it becomes a larger house or dormitory style accommodation) [24]
* The scene is set on the day they move in to the shared flat and the group work in role for an hour, establishing the characters and their inter-relationships with each other
* Each person decides along the way how much back-story they reveal
* At a pre-determined time the suicide happens
* The person who has the "S" must ensure they are alone when the time arrives and the others in the group should co-operate with this. The suicide itself must be (under) acted with no "undue dramatics"
* The others avoid witnessing the suicide but when the victim is discovered the aftermath is acted out for a further 15 minutes.

---

[24] I have since used this structure to introduce larger numbers of OYT members to serious projects such as Missing Dan Nolan and One Million to STOP THE TRAFFIK. It achieves serious responses from able performers while conveying the idea of subtle underacting.

The Story Behind - Too Much Punch For Judy by Mark Wheeller

Everyone was pleased that first morning's work and everyone bonded well. It also served as an excellent warm up to the main event.

In the afternoon I outlined my ideas for the play and went through basic blocking, as much as anything to show I was organised.

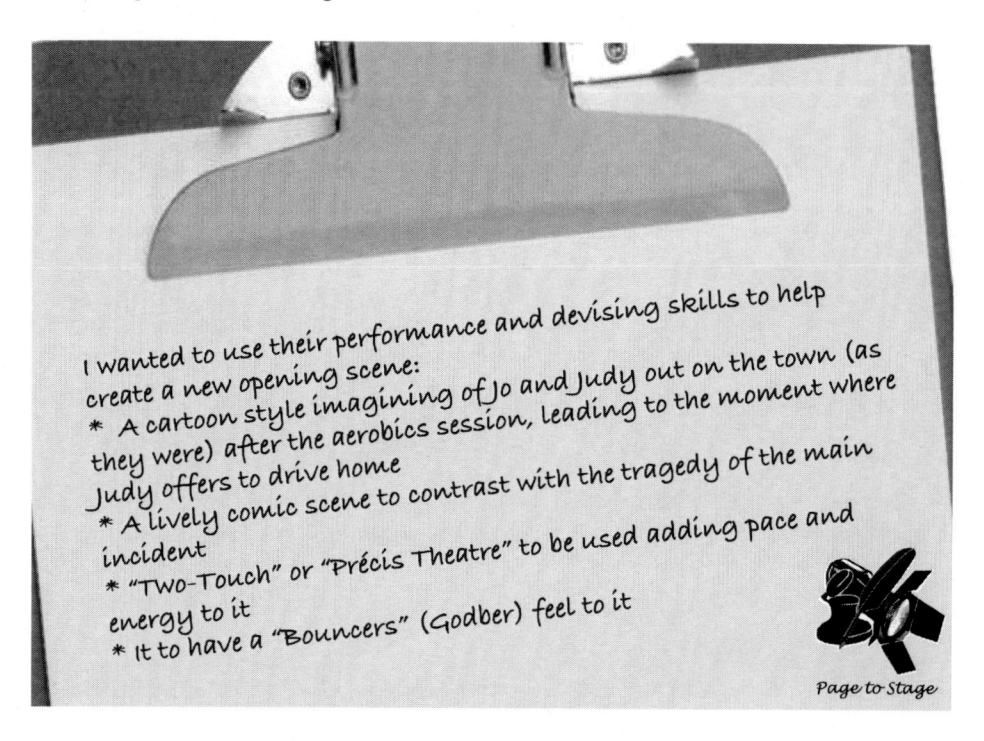

> I wanted to use their performance and devising skills to help create a new opening scene:
> * A cartoon style imagining of Jo and Judy out on the town (as they were) after the aerobics session, leading to the moment where Judy offers to drive home
> * A lively comic scene to contrast with the tragedy of the main incident
> * "Two-Touch" or "Précis Theatre" to be used adding pace and energy to it
> * It to have a "Bouncers" (Godber) feel to it

Page to Stage

Steve and Matt immediately started talking about Steven Berkoff's style of theatre. My knowledge of Berkoff was reduced to a trip in Edinburgh I had organised with EYT members aged from 12-18 to see a rare student production of "*East*". We had no warning from the venue as to the nature of the content/language, so it had been embarrassing for me with such young students. Consequently I had ignored Berkoff's stylistic genius. Steve and Matt inspired me to investigate his work. I am now a fan!

I left them to develop the scene and went off shopping!

The Story Behind - Too Much Punch For Judy by Mark Wheeller

One of my directing techniques (if that is what it can be called) has been referred to as the "cup of coffee method".

> I give the cast a particularly difficult section of script, or outline, to be developed and leave them to it while I retire somewhere else and have a cup of coffee
>
> * I may pop back into the room to see how they are progressing, but more often, I will stay away and return at a pre-determined time to cast a fresh eye on their work
>
> I have not seen professional directors working so do not know if this is a common practice. I see the function of the director as:
>
> * An enabler/facilitator rather than an instructor
>
> * Being able to recognise good ideas and using them to fashion something together that "works"
>
> * Someone who does not have a grand vision set in stone. (If I did this it would limit anyone else's input and mean that any project is restricted to the limitations of my ability)
>
> * One consequence of my way of working is that my casts have a strong sense of ownership of what they perform, even if I have "written" it

The scene the four performers devised was exactly what I was after... better actually and a huge improvement on the childish Captain Assertive scene. Their initial ideas started me off on the path to the Bob and Nob scene, although they started here as Dave and Dave.

I thought this was the final piece of the *Too Much Punch* script jigsaw!

I was wrong.

That came a year later when Alistair Black (then the Drama Adviser for Hampshire) saw the professional production at Oaklands.

The Story Behind - Too Much Punch For Judy by Mark Wheeller

He said, at the start, it had provided high energy and laughs but if we re-visited the same scene at the end, with the same high energy it would appear empty; as the audience know what happens, so they won't laugh.

He was right.

It was such a simple, yet intelligent alteration and one that is now a key part of the play's structure. Thanks Alistair!

That week with the Ape actors was great and we developed a powerful and emotive performance. David, from Touchstone, had laid down a quality starting point for the accident scene we went on to develop into a classy (as I described it in my diary) version that was, in my opinion, ground-breaking.

We were excited about our test performance at GSA on the Friday before the tour. I was intrigued to see what this "informed" audience (GSA tutors and students) would make of it. Also my fiancée (Rachael) was seeing it for the first time after having heard me talk so much about it.

It went down a storm.

Fay was exceptional, holding her own in the company of the three trained actors.

> ***Too Much Punch*** was the show that started it all for me. Matt originally told me about it at Guildford in our final year (1988). At that time you needed an Equity card to get acting work and there were only a certain amount of cards.
> By doing a TIE tour, we could get a card.
> The play gave me a grounding in everything I have done since. I knew from the start it was something extraordinary. It is a testament to its writing that it still tours to this day. The power of using verbatim language from interviews worked brilliantly in conveying the truthfulness of Judy's responses to her sister's death.
> I will never forget the power of performing it for the first time in Guildford and feeling the room become silent after the accident scene as the true horror of Judy and her sister's night out became clear.
> Seeing 17-year-old Fay Davis delivering a highly charged performance (Judy) twice a day for 3 months to audiences, who were almost the same age as her, was incredible!
> I went into ITV's ***London's Burning*** series (playing Colin Parrish) almost straight afterwards.... I owe you and Matt a big one!
> Later I co-wrote a book about Brighton & Hove Albion's fans campaign to save the club using verbatim interviews, partly inspired by my experience of doing ***Too Much Punch for Judy***, realising how powerful they can be [25]
>
> ### Steve North performer in that first Ape performance

Frank's determination to get Fay playing Judy again and his faith in Matt paid off. This production was the closest I would get to an Epping Youth Theatre "professional" tour. It proved, as John Rowley had said a year earlier, we had "missed a trick"!

---

[25] *We Want Falmer: How Brighton & Hove Albion Football Club and it's fans united to build a stadium.* Steve North and Paul Hodson (Stripe Publishing 2011)

The Story Behind - Too Much Punch For Judy by Mark Wheeller

Too Much Punch was life changing, gave me my equity card and a stepping-stone to other Theatre and TV and film jobs. It enabled me to see most counties in England, not to mention trips to Wales, Jersey and Germany.

Fay Davies 2011

The show was a foundation for everything I have done. It is amazing the number of people I have met who have been influenced by it.
A woman in her thirties stopped me in street at Great North Run and said, "Did you come to my school with a play called "Too Much Punch For Judy" some years back?"
People don't forget it.
I also met Kaye Wragg's husband at the start of the race. He said how influential it had been on her career. It made Zoe Henry (Rhona on Emmerdale) want to be an actress when she saw Ape perform it at Loughton College.

Tony Audenshaw (Bob Hope in Emmerdale – amongst other things) 2011

TOO MUCH PUNCH FOR JUDY

The Story Behind - Too Much Punch For Judy by Mark Wheeller

The production snowballed, picking up more bookings from Road Safety Departments across the UK. It seemed inconceivable that a play, which had started out in our little Drama Studio, could be such a success. If I had set out to write a successful play it would not have been about drinking and driving, that's for sure!

By May 1990 I was trying to write a hit musical.

I was convinced I'd found a subject with "hit" written all over it.

A girl who I taught had developed a GCSE exam piece about her struggle to be recognised as a footballer battling against the authorities (and her mother) to achieve her "goal".

She was on the verge of selection by the England women's team when I suggested making her story into a musical **Zigger Zagger** for girls (and boys).

Although **No Place for a Girl** has been performed on occasions up and down the country it has never become as popular as I imagined it might.

I wonder what the missing ingredient is?

Too Much Punch clearly has that ingredient.

On the 11th May 1990, I received a letter from Councillor Ken Boyden from Wellington City Council (New Zealand). He was the Chair of Wellington City Council Road Safety Committee and the New Zealand Traffic Institute Road Safety Committee. Before re-locating to New Zealand (1965) he had been a member of the Lancashire Constabulary. Ken had kept in touch and had read reports on the play when it was performed in Lancashire. He wanted to know if I would allow it to tour in New Zealand! Of course I would!!! He had a visit to the UK planned and wanted to meet with me.

My Oaklands Youth Theatre (OYT) had recently been selected to perform **Hard To Swallow** at the first **Lloyds Bank National Young Theatre Challenge**. The prize was a performance at the Royal National Theatre in London... on the Olivier stage! [26] Maureen Dunbar, mother of Catherine, whose tragic story is told in that play, was so proud of what we had achieved, that her Trust Fund generously sponsored a two week tour of schools in Texas, USA.

> To raise interest (and cash in on the success!) we mounted a revival of Too Much Punch For Judy with, in my opinion, an even better accident scene.
>
> We used scaffolding bars (the material the bridge Toni had crashed into was made from) rather than the baseball bats Ape used.

The **Too Much Punch** name helped me to sell the idea to officials in Houston.

---

(26) In the event Oaklands Youth Theatre performed Hard To Swallow on this famous stage on the day Lord Olivier passed away 11th July 1989.

The Story Behind - Too Much Punch For Judy by Mark Wheeller

As luck would have it, the week Ken was in the UK coincided with the day we had our final rehearsal of *Too Much Punch* prior to OYT's departure. Not only was I able to meet him but also he was able to see a polished production, which left an indelible impression on him.

He asked if they could set the play in New Zealand.

I remembered my lack of control with Touchstone and stood my ground saying there was no need. If the truth of the location is altered, it is on the rocky road to becoming fictionalised.

Ken returned to New Zealand and organised a national tour.

Too Much Punch became the most performed play in New Zealand for three years (with John Godber's *Bouncers* coming second!).

He secured a British Council grant for me to watch the play, run workshops and participate in question and answer sessions.

The New Zealand production, directed by Ken Duncum, had another new take on the accident scene using acrobatics. I mentioned in my diary (which I continued to write for special events) that the workshop following the production was "exceptionally funny"; a series of spontaneous comedy improvisations which focussed on how to avoid driving drunk. The Wellington Evening Post approved:

EVENING POST

Road Safety Drama Pulls no Punches

In 1983 secondary school students all over the country were bussed in at great expense to see "The Roadshow", an extravaganza to teach good driving habits. The message vanished in a mess of technical wizardry and Star Wars symbolism designed to keep teenagers from getting bored. Attention was grabbed, but hearts and minds were not engaged.

No such fate should await Too Much Punch for Judy... It avoids the horror of the accident but concentrates clearly and forthrightly on greater horrors: the burden Judy will have to bear the rest of her days and the waste of life.

There cannot be many worthier causes - and it's good theatre too!
Laurie Atkinson

The Story Behind - Too Much Punch For Judy by Mark Wheeller

Just before I left New Zealand, I was invited to participate in a TV interview and the company filming the feature hastily arranged a meeting with me. They had seen a copy of the *Too Much Punch* book. They said they were looking to make *Happy Soap* (which featured as a story in the original IAS publication) into a cartoon film! Sadly it didn't happen but it inspired *Wacky Soap (The Musical)*.

My friend Danny Sturrock, who has just completed his film degree, assures me he will make this film! Watch this space!

The play continued touring throughout the UK and developed its reputation. In October 1991, the Prince Michael of Kent Road Safety Award gave me the Special Award for Road Safety for writing it.

Mark Wheeller receives the Prince Michael Road Safety Special Award from Prince Michael of Kent.

At this time schools occasionally performed it as their GCSE exam piece, something I didn't consider for my own classes. The Institute of Alcohol Studies sold their print run of the play within a year or so, but never took up the option to reprint it. I hoped this would be a blessing in disguise, as now, with its impressive track record, I thought a mainstream publisher would adopt it.

By the end of that year it had been turned down by all of them. At least these two rejections offered some kind of reasoning for their decision. Many didn't.

The Story Behind - Too Much Punch For Judy by Mark Wheeller

> I know this will disappoint and annoy you, but our decision not to publish is based on two principal issues.
>
> * Firstly it is strongly orientated towards a TIE format rather than a conventional play
>
> * Secondly, it has already been published and we cannot risk investment in a play, which may have run a substantial part of its print life
>
> This may not be the case and I am aware that you are often approached for direction to copies. Unfortunately that is often the experience of many of our writers and the eventual production in covers too often doesn't bear witness to the interest that was believed to be around previously. Cogently the investment is probably too uncertain for a series that operates on slim profit margins.
>
> **Peter Rowlands – Series Editor CUP Act Now Series.**

Cambridge University Press went on to have considerable success when, instigated by Peter (Rowlands), they published **Hard to Swallow** (which became their second best seller in the series – first being **Gregory's Girl**).

I also enjoyed working with Andy Kempe developing **Arson About** for Nelson Thornes. It was the first time I had the opportunity to work with an editor who pushed me to develop my work. **Arson** became a rare survivor when NT were taken over by Oxford University Press. In 2017 the play was rebranded as **Butcher, Butcher Burning Bright** for their flagship **Oxford Playscripts** series.

> I have submitted the play to Andy Kempe, the series editor of our Dramascripts series for review. I am afraid that he does not consider it suitable for the series. We are looking for scripts that are longer and offer greater depth of characterisation and narrative.
>
> However Andy intends to contact you in the near future to discuss other work you have which may prove suitable for inclusion in the series.
>
> **Lisa Thomas – Commissioning Editor –Humanities.**

The Story Behind - Too Much Punch For Judy by Mark Wheeller

The nineties were frustrating for me. It appeared that I was a successful playwright but that wasn't how it seemed to me.

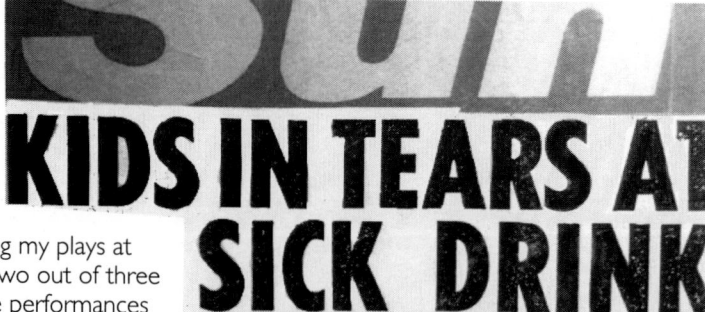

Ape were performing my plays at least twice a day in two out of three school terms but the performances were ephemeral. More often than not PSHE (Personal, Social and Health Education) teachers booked the performance. Drama teachers would not always see it.

The reaction to Ape's incredible performances were fantastic so it was they who garnered the reputation and not me.

Around this time I cheekily inserted my name into the final monologue, taken from a direct quote Toni made on TVAM. I imagine (but I don't know) Ape ignored my addition! I wasn't bitter, honest, but I was feeling frustrated by the lack of recognition!

Meanwhile in Scotland the play suddenly became controversial. Rob Fairburn of the Sun newspaper ran a "shock article", with the headline:
"Kids in Tears at Sick Drink Driving Show"

In the climax of the article he describes the "horror" that turned these young Scottish stomachs:

> "The decapitation scene is played out with red and black handkerchiefs to symbolise death."

The Story Behind - Too Much Punch For Judy by Mark Wheeller

Handkerchiefs??? This sounded nowhere near as shocking as I intended it to be.

The article was laughable and quickly forgotten!

TIE groups in England saw Ape's success and some developed their own Road Safety plays to exploit the funding. One day someone said to me: "write a Road Safety play for younger pupils. If you don't someone else will and it will probably be in your style."

I took the bait and wrote *Why did the Chicken Cross the Road?* (later simply *Chicken*). Soon Chicken was on tour,(StopWatch Theatre Company) and proved even more (commercially) successful than *Too Much Punch*. At its peak it was being performed eight times a day in UK schools, although it has not (yet), achieved success abroad.

StopWatch Theatre Company, who, based on the model of Touchstone, was resident at Oaklands, negotiated a deal with Dawn Boyfield Design Associates (dbda) to design and print a supporting educational pack (sponsored by General Accident). This was written by a colleague of mine, Mike Johns, and handed out, free to schools on the tour.

Dbda were already involved in other road safety initiatives and were keen to be on board with *Chicken*. The script, at my request, became an integral part of the pack and so, for the first time, my name (brand) was being communicated, albeit to Primary schools. The sponsorship meant there was no financial risk for dbda, Stopwatch or myself but equally no one was making money from it.

Optimistically I hoped this might lead to some kind of publishing deal for *Too Much Punch*. Schools still occasionally requested copies of the script from me and I would print off copies from my new Amstrad word processor!

I mentioned the idea of publishing *Too Much Punch* to Dawn but it didn't look promising. Dbda were a design company who were generally commissioned to produce materials rather than gamble on them.

Publishing would mean a change of direction for dbda. That seemed too much to hope for!

The Story Behind - Too Much Punch For Judy by Mark Wheeller

9. Too Much Punch For Judy - Stranger than Fiction

Toni mixed in social circles verging on "celebrity", a world away from my "teacher world". Hers seemed a more exciting world than mine. Her boyfriend, when I interviewed her, was a roadie for Chas and Dave, a successful (though not particularly my cup of tea) chart band. Although not celebrities, they were part of that world. Jo, her sister, had worked for an entertainment agency dealing with performers, so they both knew many, including Freddie (I ate my hamster) Starr.

Shortly after I moved to Southampton (1987) Toni became involved with and later married, Steve Marriott, former lead singer with the Small Faces (who were a big name) and Humble Pie (big in the US). Steve was famous, by any standards and I was always star struck when I phoned, and he answered. He was always very friendly and often asked how *Too Much Punch* was progressing, saying he hoped to see it one day. I was keen to meet him but that didn't happen.

> *I can't ever go back to that night... I realise that... so... resigned... I think that's the word... I'm resigned to the fact that it's happened. There's no way I'm suddenly a pure white character with no faults. It hasn't put me off drink. I still have a glass of wine, or half a lager... but I will never drink and drive again as long as I live... never, ever... I just couldn't do it.*
>
> *"Judy"*
> *(Toni Marriott in 1986 taken from Too Much Punch For Judy)*

On the 21st April 1991 Steve was killed.

Toni and Steve had flown back from a recording session with Peter Frampton in the US a couple of days earlier. Steve's excellent biography[27] says they were both drinking and arguing loudly on the plane home. The book, written I imagine by a Steve Marriott fan, nevertheless paints Toni as the victim. Alcohol and drugs, it said,

"... *induced Steve's schizophrenic alter ego, Melvin*".

Toni described Melvin as:

"... *violent, vicious and spiteful, a totally different man to the one I had married*".

That night, when they arrived home, the arguing became worse. A friend of Toni's arrived and attempted to calm the situation suggesting they go to a local pub for a meal. The friend describes the meal as "strained". They had more drink and customers complained about their loud and aggressive behaviour. By the end of the evening they were both "out on their feet."

Their friend, worried about leaving them alone, took them to the entertainment agent I mentioned earlier, who they both knew.

---

(27) Steve Marriott: - All Too Beautiful...: Paulo Hewitt & John Weller

The Story Behind - Too Much Punch For Judy by Mark Wheeller

The arguing continued and finally, when Toni fell asleep, Steve called a cab and left.

Toni remained unaware of her husband's departure.

An hour later he arrived home and, later that night, was killed in a house fire.

It seems the most likely scenario is that he crashed out on his bed with a lighted cigarette setting fire to his mattress. He woke up and was engulfed by smoke. In an attempt to escape, he opened a storage cupboard believing it to be his bedroom door. Firemen found him there when they arrived on the scene.

I remember reading the account of the fireman/fan in the Sunday newspaper:

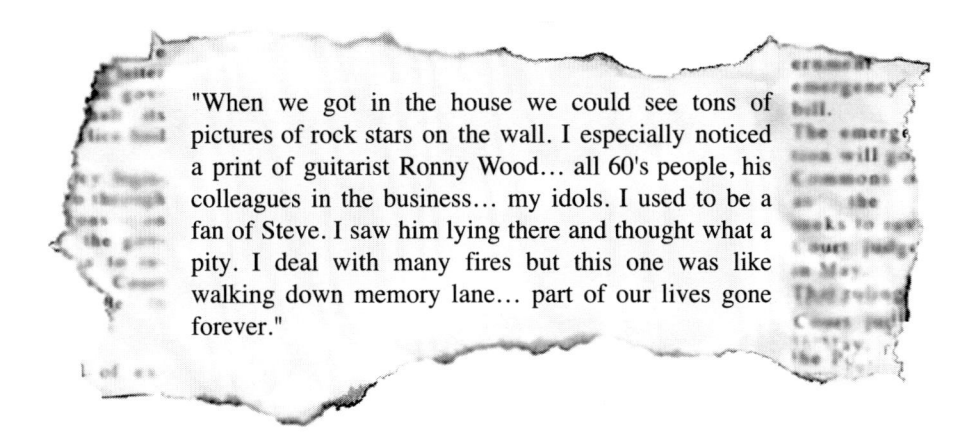

> "When we got in the house we could see tons of pictures of rock stars on the wall. I especially noticed a print of guitarist Ronny Wood... all 60's people, his colleagues in the business... my idols. I used to be a fan of Steve. I saw him lying there and thought what a pity. I deal with many fires but this one was like walking down memory lane... part of our lives gone forever."

Steve's autobiography said his blood that night contained quantities of valium, alcohol and cocaine.

This highlighted the different world Toni lived in.

This celebrity world, I perceived as exciting, also had its dark side.

Alcohol was Steve's drug of choice according to Toni.

Alcohol had led to her sister's death and now her husband's.

Within three years she became immersed in a further, unthinkable alcohol related tragedy.

If I had "written" this, no one would have believed it.

Late on the 5th October 1993 I received a phone call. Chris Caten's tone instantly told me something utterly dreadful had happened.

The Story Behind - Too Much Punch For Judy by Mark Wheeller

He informed me that Toni had been involved in a second fatal car accident on the same stretch of road where, ten years previously, she had killed Jo. She had only suffered minor injuries but the driver of the other car had died instantaneously.

The circumstances were unclear but Chris warned me there were suspicions that, once again, Toni had been drinking.

When the situation was confirmed a few days later I recorded what remains the final entry in my *Too Much Punch* diary.

> **Diary**
>
> 11th October 1993
>
> What must she have been thinking? How could she have drunk anything before driving her car after what happened to her sister and after all she said in Too Much Punch, which has now been so widely reported?
>
> Perhaps this was not the first time she has driven drunk since Jo's death.
>
> I wonder how, when and why did she change her mind? This new situation must have brought back memories of Jo. How will her involvement in the play affect the judge and jury's view? The law should be "Zero Limit" to avoid blurred edges?

Chris warned me the press would want a quote; he was right. Rather than become embroiled in interviews I prepared a press release:

> *"We are again reminded of the need for uncompromising anti-drink drive campaigning. Sadly this tragic event serves only to reinforce the importance of this message. We must all feel the deepest sympathy for the families of the innocent victims killed in drink drive accidents."*

The tragedy defied belief but in the ensuing weeks I spoke with a number of County Road Safety Officers who, shocked me by saying that the situation supported statistics:

> *"Once you have been convicted of drinking and driving you are, statistically more likely to offend again, more so than someone who has never done so!"*

The Story Behind - Too Much Punch For Judy by Mark Wheeller

Do people never learn from their mistakes?

If that was the case; could **Too Much Punch For Judy** ever affect anyone?

Have I kidded myself about its impact all this time?

Many people's attitudes, including my own, people who have performed in the play, and many who have watched it have, I believe, been affected. In my view, warnings affect people in different ways.

For example, I was dissuaded from ever taking drugs by a hard-hitting TV film, "**Gale is Dead**". That would possibly be deemed too shocking to use in Health Education programmes these days, but it worked for me. Perhaps, for others, it hadn't.

I am convinced that a range of means need to be used to convey messages such as these, including shock tactics.

I recorded my fears for the future of the play in my final diary entry:

> I have considered many things that might upset the success of the play (i.e. an actor being charged for drunk driving) and fleetingly considered (and immediately dismissed) the idea of Toni doing it again. I never imagined there would be a second death at her hands.
>
> Although it seems wrong or insensitive to be writing/thinking this; I am concerned the play will no longer pick up bookings and possibly lose existing ones. There is a cottage industry surrounding this play, a theatre company with a team of actors whose working lives are dependent on it.
>
> I wonder now how Toni views it. I have no intention of contacting her, but would respond if she phones me. I don't think she will though!
>
> The royalty situation set up in good faith all those years ago is now unacceptable and totally inappropriate."

The Story Behind - Too Much Punch For Judy by Mark Wheeller

I had agreed a royalty with Toni after discovering I was to be paid for the Scottish tour. She had been uncomfortable about it but I pushed; after all it was her story. I had no idea it may compromise her either then or the future, it just seemed "right". There was no contract; it was agreed as "friends". What had seemed appropriate at the time suddenly, in this new context seemed very wrong. I needed to talk to her about it but, realised, it may not be her top priority… or would it? In the light of the pending court case it may not reflect well on her; I phoned her and was sufficiently anxious about what I should say that I handwrote out this guide to help our conversation, which I stuck in my diary:

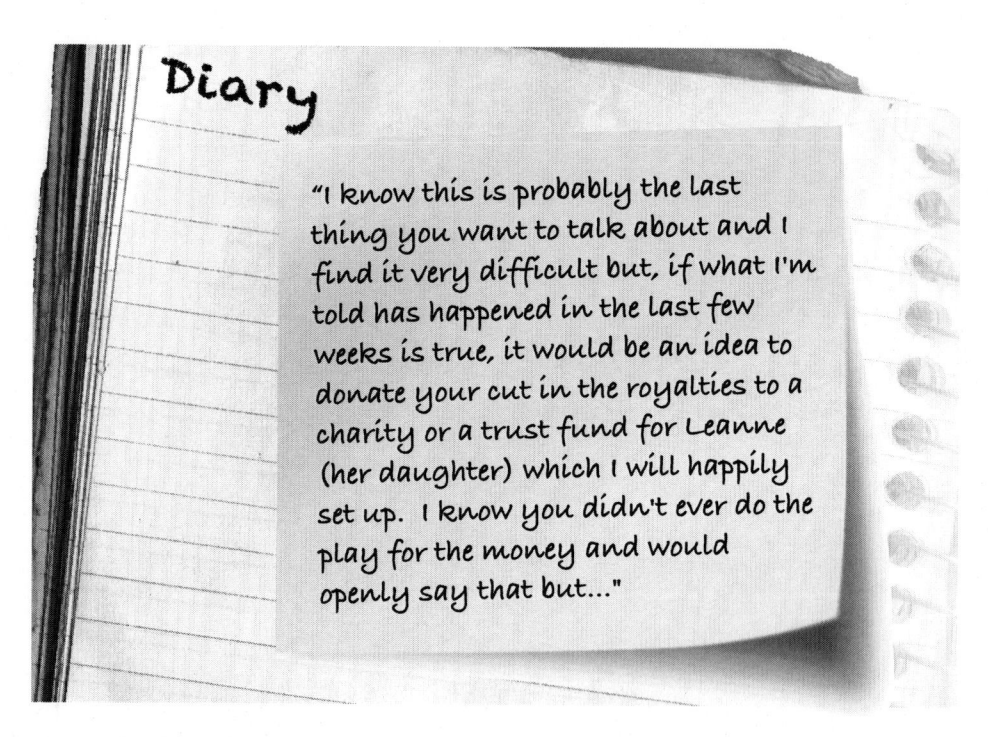

> **Diary**
>
> "I know this is probably the last thing you want to talk about and I find it very difficult but, if what I'm told has happened in the last few weeks is true, it would be an idea to donate your cut in the royalties to a charity or a trust fund for Leanne (her daughter) which I will happily set up. I know you didn't ever do the play for the money and would openly say that but…"

She was happy to discuss it but wanted to do so face to face.

I am a very black and white person. In this situation I felt it was wrong to talk to her, as my view was that drinking and driving is wrong. By talking to her I feared it would seem as though I was supporting her. The royalty situation forced me to meet her, something I would never have done otherwise.

My meeting with Toni made me understand something my wife had often said to me:

> *"Mark, there are shades of grey in most situations."*

The Story Behind - Too Much Punch For Judy by Mark Wheeller

I rang the doorbell at Toni's house. She opened her door and when she saw me, started to cry. My natural instinct was to hug her. I found myself hugging this woman who had done something so wrong; this woman I felt uncomfortable associating with. However, I realised this "woman" was still the Toni that I had known and liked, we'd got to know one another and become friends, during my final years in Epping. I found I still liked her, despite what she had done. It wasn't as though she was doing it there and then right in front of me! During our conversation I came to admire how she was coping with such an impossible situation.

As we talked, I realised why I had liked her. I liked her open and honest approach and was reminded of how she was in the original interviews. She held her hands up to what she had done, just like before. She expressed fears about going to prison but knew it was inevitable. She was desperately unhappy. She was also a victim of these tragic circumstances, something I had not appreciated prior to the visit; a shade of grey; a moment of clarity for me.

The royalty situation was resolved fast. Her royalties would go into a trust fund for her daughter, administered by Chris Caten. Toni expressed no reservation about the play continuing which took me by surprise and moreover she was keen for me to add a section telling the tragedy of the second accident.

I had not wanted Toni to think I was setting out to get another interview so had made a positive decision not to bring a tape recorder. This was not the premise for our meeting. Suddenly I was "missing an opportunity". I tentatively suggested that to be able to do this I would need to make notes:

"Would it be alright if I borrowed some paper and a pen?"

We did a brief interview; it really was brief, as it was late in the day and very much an afterthought. I noted down what I could on a little paper bag I tore apart.

I felt more intrusive than ever I had done previously.

Toni talked openly. Some of what she said at that time appears in the opening section of the current version of the play.

As I left, Toni told me she was receiving alcohol counselling a few miles from her house.

"How do you get there?" I asked imagining she would reply, "A lift from a friend".

She pointed to the car parked in front of mine.

"You're allowed to?" I ventured.

"Yes."

The ban would only take effect when she was sentenced. Sentencing took place seven and a half months after the crash. Madness!

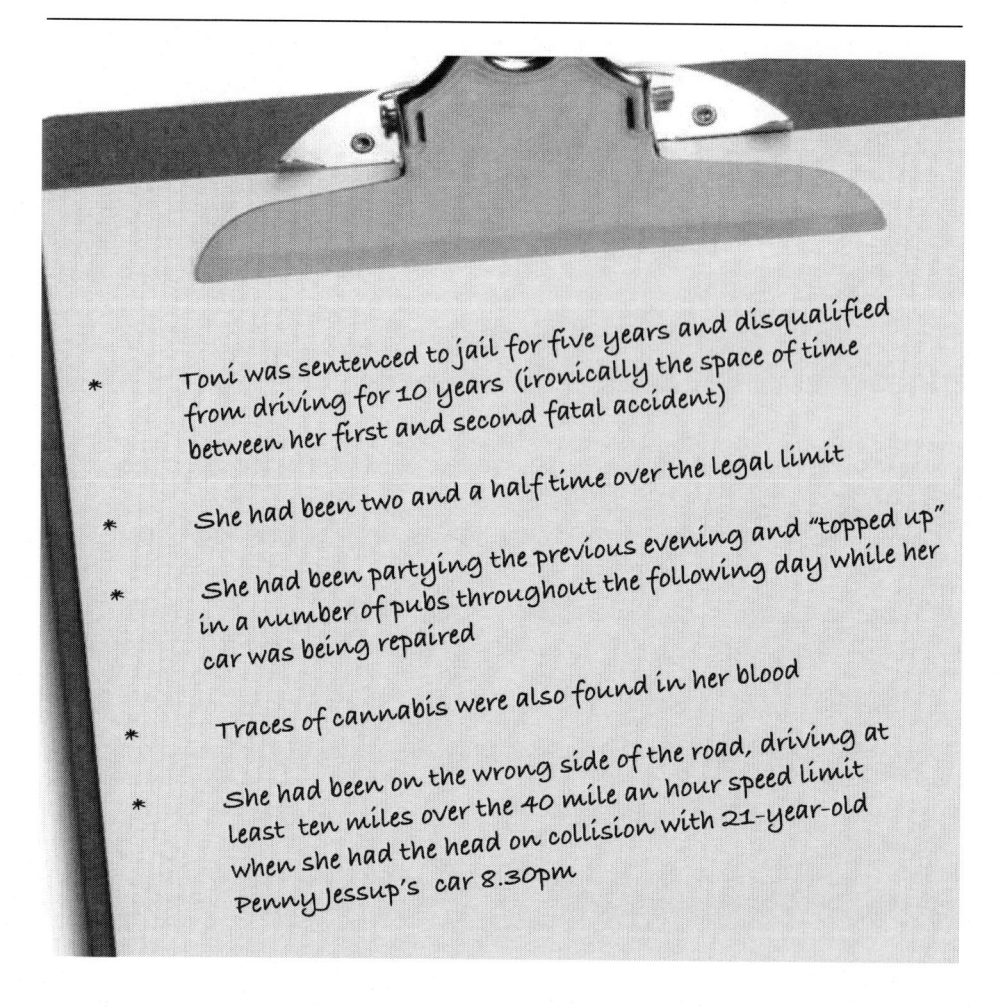

The Story Behind - Too Much Punch For Judy by Mark Wheeller

* Toni was sentenced to jail for five years and disqualified from driving for 10 years (ironically the space of time between her first and second fatal accident)

* She had been two and a half time over the legal limit

* She had been partying the previous evening and "topped up" in a number of pubs throughout the following day while her car was being repaired

* Traces of cannabis were also found in her blood

* She had been on the wrong side of the road, driving at least ten miles over the 40 mile an hour speed limit when she had the head on collision with 21-year-old Penny Jessup's car 8.30pm

The judge said that Toni had not learnt anything from her previous fatal accident.

"Although that offence occurred over 10 years ago, I would be failing in my duty if I ignored it. I am satisfied you have shown yourself to be a menace and a danger to the public, brought about, in my view, because of your drinking problems.
By your irresponsible behaviour, you abruptly brought to an end the life of a young woman of 21, causing those near to her and, in particular her parents, untold pain, suffering and misery which they will have to live with for a very long time."

The Story Behind - Too Much Punch For Judy by Mark Wheeller

The victim's parents were furious. Her father was reported as saying:

> "The Judge said she is a danger to the public and will remain a danger as long as they condone her being behind a steering wheel. I would have liked her to be put in prison and the key thrown away, but I accept that is not reasonable. She has stolen 50 or 60 years, potentially, of Penny's life and given us a life sentence. We will never, ever forget what she has done.
> We want random breath tests, manslaughter charges for drink-drivers who kill and the automatic and immediate surrender of driving licenses once the holder gives a positive breath test."

I understand Toni was sent to Holloway Prison.

I felt for her on the day the announcement was made; it was on the main news and was front page in some newspapers. I knew how scared she would have been.

I have had no contact with her since that last meeting and I am sad about that. I would love to know how she is.

When I saw her she seemed determined to sort her life out. I remember her saying the first half hadn't been successful (or happy) and she was determined that the second would be better. Certainly the prison system didn't, from what I have heard, help in the first instance. I have no idea how I came by this information (perhaps Chris Caten) but, apparently, as soon as she arrived in prison they (not Toni) decided to discontinue the alcohol counselling. I would have thought, having her as a captive and willing audience, she would be given every chance of continuing with it. As Dickens (in the guise of Mr Bumble) once said: "The law is an ass"!

After deciding to include something about the second accident in the play I made contact with Penny's family, using Chris Caten once again as the middleman. It was always good to see Chris; he typified the old style village bobby. He was, I know, proud of his involvement in *Too Much Punch* and occasionally made appearances in schools when it was performed over the years. Again, if I were ever visiting Epping, Chris is one of the people I would often search out. He was, as I hope is conveyed in the play, a true gentleman.[28]

I arrived at Penny's house. The family were gathered together: her parents, Ian, Penny's boyfriend and his sister with her husband. They told me that at one point they had wanted to stop the play but had been dissuaded by Chris who explained how much good it was doing.

---

(28) I am sad to report that Chris died following a battle against cancer in 2006.

The Story Behind - Too Much Punch For Judy by Mark Wheeller

By the time I arrived, they had decided that putting their side of the story forward could only do good for the anti drink-driving cause. I admit I felt awkward, almost disloyal. I had never taken Toni's side but did empathise with her new situation. Understandably, the whole situation for the Jessup's was far more difficult. They spoke eloquently and passionately. I felt for them and their loss; it was an incredibly raw and emotional evening. I left with some highly emotive material to fashion into a new scene for the play.

I typed out the testimony and was about to start work when I received a phone call. It was Penny's father. He wanted me to tell him the situation regarding Toni and the royalties, which I did. He was appalled and immediately withdrew permission for me to use any of the words from their interview.

To put it emotively, it looked like Toni and I had a "dirty little secret", which Penny's family had uncovered, probably by asking Chris, who was the only other person who knew. It was embarrassing and worrying. I didn't want to get myself into trouble and realised more importantly that it would look bad for Toni. Why hadn't we gone down the route of giving her royalties to charity? The truth is we were so in agreement about the fact that she should not receive them that we went for the first option of creating a trust fund for her daughter without much discussion. When I asked Chris and he hadn't offered any reservations, the assumption was that it was a good and moral solution.

Toni was, by this time, in prison so I spoke to her solicitor. It was decided that, from that point, any income due to her would go direct to the Counseling service that had helped her in Harlow. I informed Penny's father but, understandably it was too late; trust had been broken. He said I should use only quotes from their family that were already in the public domain.

I mixed those quotes with the notes I took during my final meeting with Toni to create the most recent opening section for the play. It was frustrating as the family had expressed more powerful feelings in the interview, which I feel better served their cause than the few words I was allowed to use. On the plus side, it didn't take me long to put this scene together.

Amazingly, bookings for the play continued. The program in schools became stronger. The workshop focused the audience on deciding/guessing the sentencing following her first accident. The actual sentencing is then revealed. With a true life story there is a definitive answer.

Toni was banned for 18 months and fined £250. She was also asked to pay for the damage to the bridge.

The Story Behind - Too Much Punch For Judy by Mark Wheeller

Then there is a heated debate about the rights and wrongs of that sentence.

Finally, the details of the second accident are revealed through a presentation of the Epilogue.

The audience are invariably stunned… not into silence but to outrage!

To engender some empathy for Judy, I gave the actor playing Judy these words from that interview I referred to earlier:

My inability to cope with the problems of my life, has led to someone else suffering so I have voluntarily gone into counseling with a determination to be rehabilitated back to life. I must replace drink with something else in my life.

Penny's dad is given the words he said outside the court (quoted previously), which instigates a lively debate and powerful indictment against drunk driving.

It is Toni's story and, remembering an earlier decision I made regarding the end of the play, she is given the last word:

Someone said to me that I should write to her parents to say I'm sorry but it goes beyond that doesn't it?

This provides a very different, less didactic ending, than the original:

I will never drink and drive again.

Although I like the power of that, I prefer the grey area of the genuine question Toni was facing the last time I saw her.

Should she write a letter to Penny's parents? Would you have done so?

The Story Behind - Too Much Punch For Judy by Mark Wheeller

10. Too Much Punch For Judy - Family Tree

There have been many proposals regarding *Too Much Punch* being made into a film but none have come to fruition.

Its success has led to my gaining commissions to write other material.

I am so grateful to it for opening these doors for me.

The first was in 1993.

Completely out of the blue, I had a phone call from Mandy Rigault, an Oxford Road Safety Officer. She had been impressed by *Chicken* during its Oxfordshire tour and wanted to commission a play about the dangers of speeding. Funding was secured from LARSOA (Local Authorities Road Safety Officers Association)(29) and for the first time, I was paid to write a play!

> And by the way, everything in life is writable about if you have the outgoing guts to do it and the imagination to improvise. The worst enemy to creativity is self-doubt.
> **Sylvia Plath**

I seized the opportunity, even though I knew I would have to find yet another way of staging a car accident! Eek!

Mandy took me to an open prison to conduct interviews with potential subjects. I spoke to four or five men (yes, they were all men) who had been convicted of speeding. By lunchtime I was anxious, as all the interviewees were also drunk drivers. I feared this new play might end up being a repeat of *Too Much Punch*.

In the afternoon a well-spoken man arrived saying he wanted to tell his story anonymously.

He had not been drinking but had been driving at nearly twice the legal speed limit and killed a motorcyclist who was pulling out of a garage.

This man was furious with the authorities for putting him in prison as he felt it was predominantly the fault of the motorcyclist who, he claimed, was not looking!

His lack of remorse gave me an interesting vehicle for what was to become my main character in *Legal Weapon*, Andy.

I was determined to use the strengths and authenticity of *Punch* but wanted to fuse it with a self-imposed pressure to create an original story, as I had proved able to do with *Chicken*.

---

(29) Now known as Road Safety Great Britain.

The Story Behind - Too Much Punch For Judy by Mark Wheeller

I worked around the framework of a love triangle and used the powerful words from "Andy's" testimony for the story of the accident itself. As he was speaking anonymously, I was forced to change some details to protect his identity.

Its success, live, was due to the development of an idea by Matt Allen of Ape Theatre Company that I hinted at in stage instructions for the opening scene:

"Clowns/Masks enter accompanied by appropriate pre-recorded or live music, vocal sound effects and/or gobbledygook speech. Feel free to develop this opening idea to start off with a bang!"

Matt used amplified vocal sound effects to both comic and dramatic effect throughout the whole production.

Soon after this I put myself forward for another opportunity to broaden my writing:

Tufty, a story I had read in a comic when I was a child, was being re-launched. I contacted RoSPA (Royal Society for the Prevention of Accidents) who owned the rights to *Tufty* and offered to write a musical, as it seemed the books were all sewn up!

I was called to a meeting in their Birmingham office to discuss my idea. I remember my ideas of him becoming *Tuff Tee* (street squirrel) were met with blank faces. However, something I said must have impressed them. They said they would consider a musical, but more significantly they set me a homework:

* To write a 700-word story to a strict "brief"

They said they wanted to consider commissioning me to write stories for a third book, which at that point had not been commissioned. My wife, Rachael, is an infant school trained English specialist so, we joined forces, and came up with our first story, *Tufty and the Drums*.

142

The Story Behind - Too Much Punch For Judy by Mark Wheeller

Within a week RoSPA contracted us to write their third and final, book for the re-launch saying they were excited about the "life" we might bring to the project. We were both thrilled to be involved in something that had a childhood connection to us. We had to write 12 stories in one month, one every three days! We decided to write some together and some separately to help us to meet the challenging deadline. Unfortunately this coincided with OYT preparing for a performance of *Chunnel of Love* at the National Student Drama Festival. Yes, one of my productions was showcased at the NSDF![30]

It was a very busy month spending many late nights on the stories. We had a four year old and a two year old (Ollie and Charlie) and many of the stories were based on our experiences with them. We finished the book on time and it was published fast.[31]

We were subsequently commissioned to write one story a month for a comic that ran for a further year. We would not see the finished product until we dashed over to Sainsbury's on the release day having set the illustrators gentle challenges, such as casting the Crossing Patrol man (a hedgehog!) as a magical genie in a Pantomime for the Xmas edition!

Without *Too Much Punch* I would never have thought of putting myself forward for, or having the experience to land, the *Tufty* job. I really had become Mr Road Safety Writerman!

Other commissions did come along… but not for a while.

---

(30) *Oaklands Youth Theatre, under my direction, was selected to perform Chunnel of Love (my bi-lingual play, co-written with Graham Cole, about an unplanned teenage pregnancy, now published by Zig Zag) at the NSDF. Although we were slated in some of the (vicious) reviews, Lizzie Hole won a nomination for Best Actress at the Festival. Two subsequent productions I have directed were also entered. Neither was selected, but Missing Dan Nolan was shortlisted. A few years ago the NSDF altered their rules so that productions including under 16's are no longer eligible. I view this as a retrograde step and it has prevented me from entering productions since that date. I hope they reconsider this decision.*

(31) *Tufty's Adventures published by RoSPA is available from Amazon and other good bookshops.*

The Story Behind - Too Much Punch For Judy by Mark Wheeller

By 1994 two of my scripts had been published. Neither were road safety plays: *Hard to Swallow*[32] and *Race to Be Seen*. *Hard to Swallow* was beginning to be used by school drama departments, possibly on the back of the success of the book and TV film *Catherine*, but *Race* was "remaindered" soon after, along with the most of the Longman Imprint series.

It seemed increasingly unlikely in 1994 that any publisher would be prepared to publish *Too Much Punch For Judy*, despite its successful record as a touring production. I remained certain there was a market for it and determined to seek out opportunities.

---

(32) Hard to Swallow became a set text on the Eduqas GCSE Drama spec to be taught from 2016. The full production dvd is available from Wheellerplays@gmail.com

11. Too Much Punch For Judy -
Back to School

My plays, including *Too Much Punch For Judy*, remained unavailable for schools in published form for a further five years. My three road safety plays were each being performed at least twice a day, every day of the autumn and spring terms, across the UK and New Zealand. I alerted publishers to this but no one expressed any interest.

No one showed any interest... apart from dbda.

By 1997 the General Accident money sponsoring *Chicken* had run out. On my advice dbda had reduced the size of the published script from an A4 glossy pamphlet to a rehearsal friendly A5 size script and printed it on matt paper.

> This was an aurally, visually and dramatically shocking depiction of the danger of drink driving. The Ape Theatre cast was absolutely brilliant. They had our students laughing one minute and crying the next. This was worth ten classroom lectures and if the message the play offered didn't get through with this show, it never will.
>
> Geoff Carr - Deputy Head teacher at Francis Combe Community School &College

Obviously a few extra copies of the script that they had, sold sufficiently well for Dawn to finally submit to my bleating on about how schools really did also, "want to get hold of copies of *Too Much Punch For Judy*... ooh and *Legal Weapon*". She realised that she might be able to use the network of County Council Road Safety Education Liaison Officers to promote the scripts into schools.

In 1999 dbda published my road safety trilogy as separate scripts.

I took the opportunity to go through all the testimony for *Too Much Punch* and added little bits here and there. I also reconsidered the use of swear words which I had removed with a heavy heart back in 1987. I felt their inclusion offered some important clues about how to play Judy on stage.

One of the plays I saw most in the late 90s as a GCSE examiner was *Bouncers* (which had been written a few years before *Punch*). When I originally saw it in Edinburgh (1984) I could not imagine being allowed to present it in a secondary school as it had so much "bad language". By the end of the century it became a staple part of the GCSE curriculum, revered by Drama teachers and considered "grown up" by students.

Many schools have become more enlightened, as illustrated by a recent contribution to a thread on the TES drama teachers' forum about the censorship of bad language in school plays.

The Story Behind - Too Much Punch For Judy by Mark Wheeller

> If you limit your school play to those without bad language, you are VERY limited, especially in this day and age where most contemporary plays will have some form of swearing. You will limit yourself to dated plays or those written specifically for schools, which I generally hate.
> If you played most 'classics' in accordance with their sub-text you would find much 'darker' material - even if you took something like 'A Doll's House' or 'Antigone' - no swearing as such, but is the subject matter any more appropriate than the F word? Drama, in general is 'challenging'. It depends on your school of thought, but for me, I like my school plays to make the audience think and to try to have an emotional impact - I like to raise issues.
> If I were to compare it to other subjects, I would say it would be like a scientist avoiding teaching things like genetic modification or cloning or abortion simply because they are contentious.
> **Bethany Dawson. Head of Drama at Emanuel School in Battersea**

If I am asked for permission to cut these words, I always say yes. I would far rather the message is conveyed, albeit in a slightly diluted form, than not at all.

I also scripted the Bob and Nob scene (I amused myself with their cheeky names) developing it from the Ape version of 1987 and the improvised OYT Houston tour version created in 1990. My wife Rachael also helped, as I wasn't happy with how I'd written Jo and Judy's lines! Whenever I hear the section that includes the lines "*Tramped up we are*" I always think of her as she wrote that (until now, never credited – apologies)!

One other speech I remember discovering when I re-read the testimony was a section I must have decided was too graphic back in 1987.

"When they started to get her (Jo out of the car, I had to keep members of the public who'd come out to watch away from the scene as it wasn't a pretty sight. They realised she had severe injuries so they had to… somebody got some plastic bags which they put over her head and shoulders… just to make it a little bit better for people that were gathered around."

This was a section I added to the revised script partly because I was aware that the actor playing PC Abrahams did not have much to get his teeth into. The graphic nature of what he was describing, combined with his attempts to say it "decently", come across as so authentic.

The other major alteration to that (year 2000) published version was the inclusion of an epilogue adding the true tragic twist of the second incident to the play.

Punch and *Legal* were published in 1999 joining *Chicken* in the dbda "catalogue". Gradually word spread from RSO's and my own newly developed "Wheellerplays" (note the two e's and two l's) web site.

These plays, that were being performed so regularly in schools by professional TIE companies, were now finally available in script form for school students to perform.

The Story Behind - Too Much Punch For Judy by Mark Wheeller

Within two years **Punch** became one of the most popular Drama GCSE scripts for study and performance (alongside **Bouncers** and **Blood Brothers**) in GCSE Drama exams.

Teachers told me about delegates (and senior examiners) openly complimenting their "accessibility" at exam training sessions.

There was one Edexcel conference I attended where the tutor was asking for suggestions from the floor about plays that had worked for teacher delegates. My name was mentioned as a playwright and one man piped up:

"If anyone else mentioned Mark bloody Wheeller again; I shall leave!"

Later, we were sat in small groups introducing ourselves to each other. When it came to me, I said my name with a cheeky smile and glanced at the man. Everyone sniggered and afterwards the two of us chatted. He explained that my plays were being repeatedly recommended at conferences he attended. He hadn't read any (no idea why, if they were being recommended so much!) but was fed up hearing my name. I trust one day he will investigate at least one of my plays!

I had never thought students in my school should use my plays for GCSE exams perceiving them purely as YT productions. It wasn't until a newly appointed colleague, Johnny Carrington, suggested we use them in exams that I saw their potential for securing better (or safer?) exam results.

I am embarrassed to admit that we subsequently went to the other extreme and took full advantage of my being a unique resource in our department.

It took over 10 years for **Too Much Punch** to find its way back into students performance repertoire, but now, I am proud to say it seems to have become part of the fabric of many UK Drama departments.

It continues to outsell any of my other scripts (apart from those that are now set texts), selling many more, in a year, as my other plays put together!

Inspired by its success I returned to using the purist documentary form to write **Missing Dan Nolan** in 2002.[33]

Like **Too Much Punch**, the words of the people involved with Dan's tragic disappearance was, I felt, the only way to tell this tragic story. Their words are so much more powerful than any invention of mine could ever be.

I found I really enjoyed the process of jig sawing these words together and, having constructed fictional plays of my own, felt more expert in experimenting with chronology and form. Structurally, **Dan** is more complex than **Too Much Punch** and along with **Graham** (which tells the story of writing the original **Race To Be Seen** play), is my favourite of my own plays!

---

[33] *Missing Dan Nolan tells the tragic story of Dan's disappearance after a nights fishing in Hamble, Hampshire. It is told using the words of his family, friends and the policeman in charge of the resulting investigation. The script is published by zincpublishing.co.uk and in 2016 it became a Set text for the OCR GCSE Drama exam. The full production dvd is available from Wheellerplays@gmail.com*

The Story Behind - Too Much Punch For Judy by Mark Wheeller

Another commission came along in 2008 to write a play about safety on buses. I collaborated on this with Danny Sturrock. He wrote the lines for the two young people and I for the two older characters. It was a great way to collaborate with someone whose work I really admire and ensured the voices of the two sets of characters in the play are truly different.

Driven to Distraction [34] toured secondary schools for a while and is now published by dbda. It has recently become much more current given the revelations about Jimmy Savile.

I never thought I'd write another road safety play but, events in real life led to a reappraisal not to mention my most far flung commission! Chris Gilfoy was a performer/deviser in the first production of **Chicken**, giving his name to the central character. He became a stalwart OYT member and in 2004 became a World Champion Banger Racer! In 2007 he was seriously injured in a tragic car accident and has never fully recovered.

One day students arrived at my Drama lesson saying they'd never heard anything so sad in all their lives. He'd talked to them as part of a road safety project. So, when I was commissioned to write a play of my own choosing by the Victoria Academy Shanghai (Hong Kong) I wrote a verbatim account of his story… thus was born my final road safety play; **Chequered Flags to Chequered Futures**. Chris and I travelled to HK to watch this extraordinary production. The cast could not believe that they were meeting the real Chris Gilfoy. What a project!

Chris is still battling towards a recovery and has a powerful story to tell that will, I hope, inspire yet another way of staging a car accident!

Too Much Punch has taken a highly irregular journey.

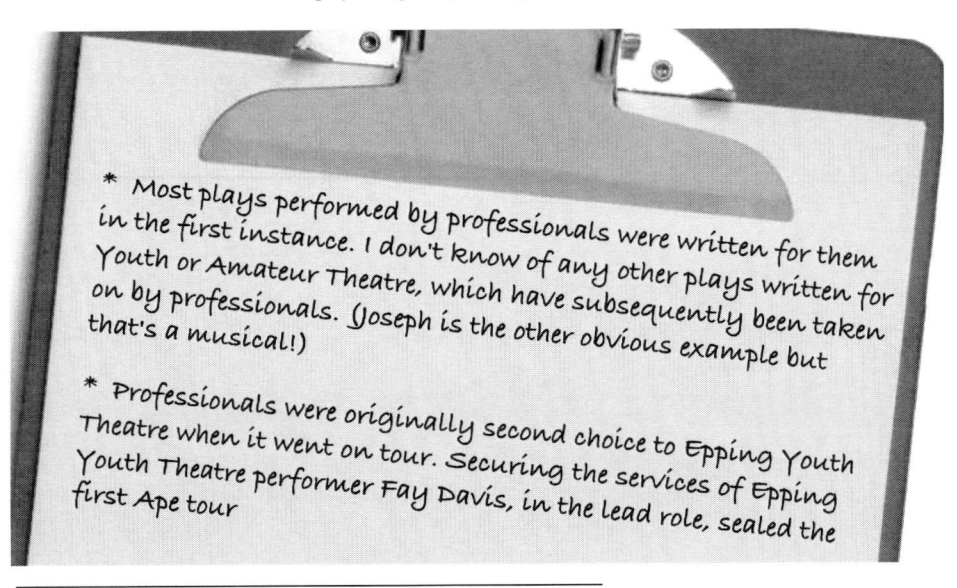

> * Most plays performed by professionals were written for them in the first instance. I don't know of any other plays written for Youth or Amateur Theatre, which have subsequently been taken on by professionals. (Joseph is the other obvious example but that's a musical!)
>
> * Professionals were originally second choice to Epping Youth Theatre when it went on tour. Securing the services of Epping Youth Theatre performer Fay Davis, in the lead role, sealed the first Ape tour

---

(34) The Driven to Distraction and CF2CF scripts are published by zincpublishing.co.uk and the full production dvd of CF2CF is available on a double disc with Chicken from Wheellerplays@gmail.com

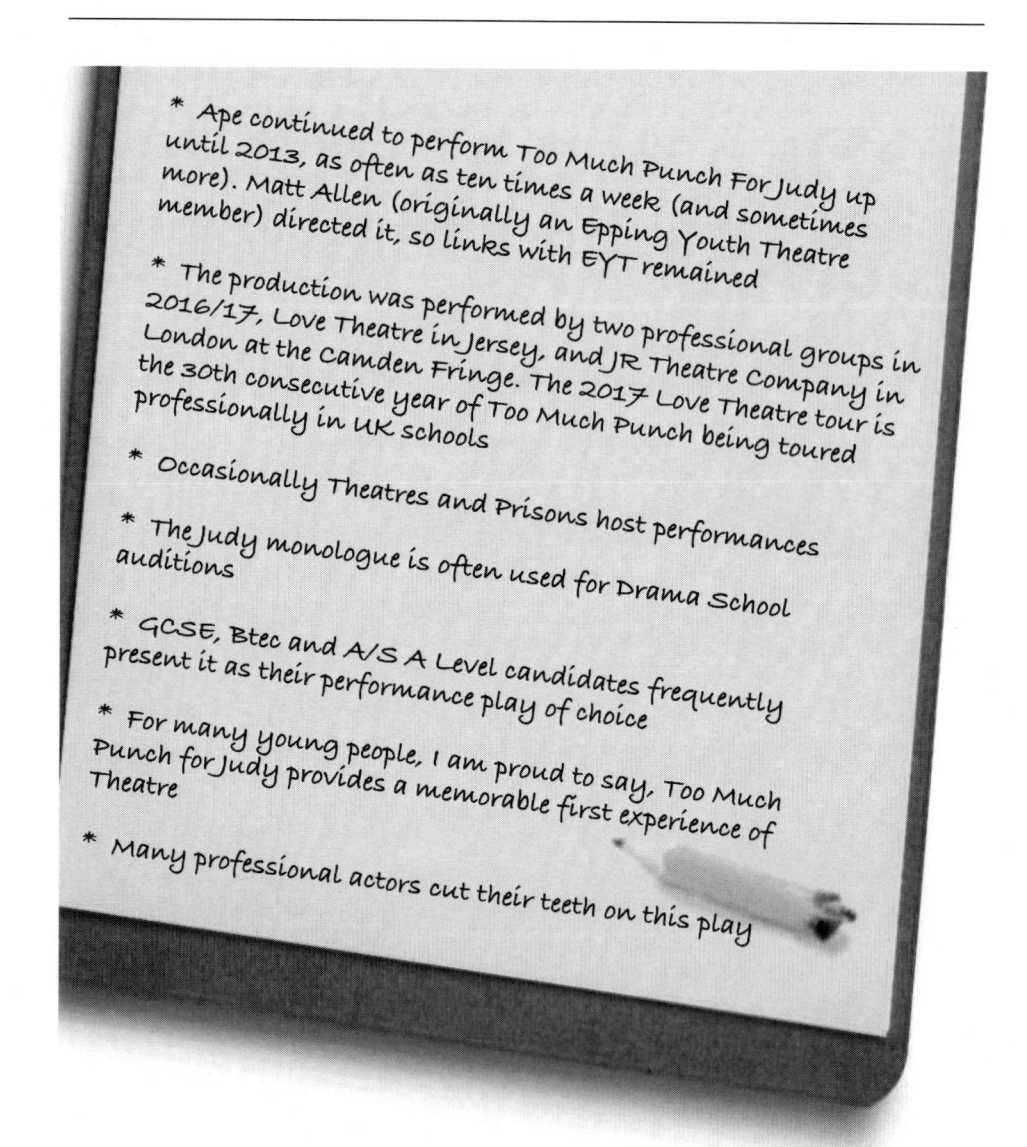

The Story Behind - Too Much Punch For Judy by Mark Wheeller

* Ape continued to perform Too Much Punch For Judy up until 2013, as often as ten times a week (and sometimes more). Matt Allen (originally an Epping Youth Theatre member) directed it, so links with EYT remained

* The production was performed by two professional groups in 2016/17, Love Theatre in Jersey, and JR Theatre Company in London at the Camden Fringe. The 2017 Love Theatre tour is the 30th consecutive year of Too Much Punch being toured professionally in UK schools

* Occasionally Theatres and Prisons host performances

* The Judy monologue is often used for Drama School auditions

* GCSE, Btec and A/S A Level candidates frequently present it as their performance play of choice

* For many young people, I am proud to say, Too Much Punch for Judy provides a memorable first experience of Theatre

* Many professional actors cut their teeth on this play

The highlights of my Christmas television viewing (2011) were the new BBC adaptations of **Great Expectations** and **The Borrowers.** The star of both of these was one such actor, Shaun Dooley, who played the Blacksmith and Pod respectively. On one evening while proofing this second edition I also spotted Shaun in the BBC Gunpowder (about Guy Faulkes) as Sir William Wade. He was also Rickie Gillespie in Series 2 of Broadchurch. He's doing well!

The Story Behind - Too Much Punch For Judy by Mark Wheeller

Many more regularly feature in television work. *Corrie* and *Emmerdale* sent scouts to Ape's productions, just look at this list I culled from www.apetheatrecompany.co.uk

> Kaye Wragg (*Lady Jane, The Lakes, Coronation Street, Slap, Born to Run*); Tony Audenshaw (*Peak Practice, Brookside, Prime Suspect, and Emmerdale*); Sara Bienvenu (*West End The Graduate*); Paul McGreevy, Dawn Finnerty (*Manchester's Royal Exchange*); Nick Gallagher (*Casualty*, thanks directly to casting director Sue Caitliffe seeing the show); Sean Gleeson (*Eastenders*, West End with *The Wier*), Julian Kerridge (*Dangerfield, Breaking the Code, Killing Me Softly*); Shaun Dooley (*Dalziel and Pascoe, Coronation Street*, the Vicar in *Eastenders, Warriors*, National Theatre *Brassed Off*); Stephen North (ITV's *London's Burning*, national tour of *Fever Pitch, The Bill* and *The Day Britain Stopped*), Matt Kane (*Buddy, Sweat* and *Cabaret* all West End, numerous number one tours, starring role in *The K Hole*, writer and director for *Beautiful People* and *Pills, Thrills @ Automobiles*); Matt Robinson in the Tribe series shot in New Zealand; Dan Jarvis (*EastEnders*), Esther McAuley the National Theatre, and many, many more.

It is not only from the professional productions that successful people in the world of entertainment have emerged.

Twenty years after that first performance in converted converted classroom, I sat in a Southampton cinema with my family to see a wonderful new film written and directed by Garth Jennings, Epping Youth Theatre's sound guy for *Too Much Punch*.

Garth's film was *Son Of Rambow*.

It even had a nod to our school, as the school featured in the film is called St. Johns.

Garth was nominated for a **BAFTA** as Best Newcomer.

Garth also directed the 2005 **'The Hitchhiker's Guide to the Galaxy'** and subsequently wrote and directed a full-animated film **'SING'** (2016) distributed by Universal Pictures no less!

The Story Behind - Too Much Punch For Judy by Mark Wheeller

I have remained in touch with many from the Epping Youth Theatre cast.

Barrie Sapsford and I have remained in regular contact since that time, meeting up to see occasional West End productions. Latterly we have worked together as his company filmed high quality DVDs of OYT's recent productions (Graham and One Million to STOP THE TRAFFIK) and he has designed this book.

I was sad to lose touch with those who were crucial to that major success in my life. However, with the advent of Facebook, I have enjoyed regaining contact with many of them. In some cases we have re-established a lasting and on-going friendship. Consequently I have shared drafts of this book with them. When I sent an early version to Jodi (the youngest member of EYT), I was concerned, as I feared she might be offended that I hadn't mentioned her that much. When I sent her a text warning her, she immediately messaged back:

It is good to know that they (or at least she) also valued the strength of the relationships we all shared. To me they were as important as any product to come out of those years. They stand as proof to me that positive informal relationships in an educational context will in the right hands lead to outstanding work being produced that will be remembered fondly by all who participated.

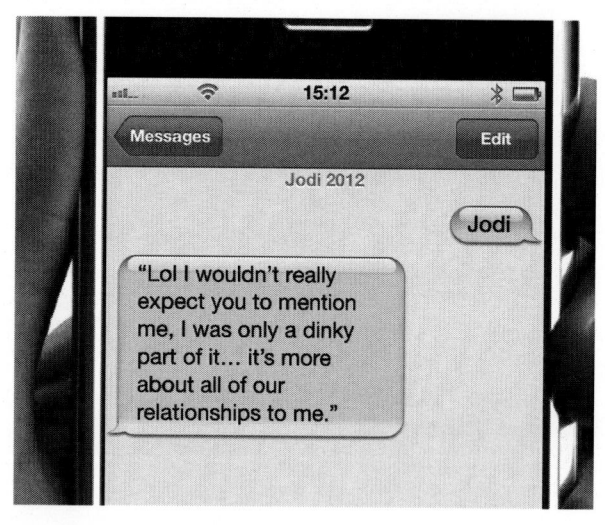

"Lol I wouldn't really expect you to mention me, I was only a dinky part of it... it's more about all of our relationships to me."

I am so thankful that the internet (and Facebook especially) has helped to reignite most of those very special relationships.

Left to Right: Jodi - Barrie - Mark - Fay Summer 2012

The Story Behind - Too Much Punch For Judy by Mark Wheeller

Appendix: - Staging the Accident

If you stage *Too Much Punch For Judy* you cannot shy away from the fact that the key moment is the accident scene.

This scene gave me sleepless nights and many rehearsals full of struggle and a fear that I would never find a way of staging it effectively.

You can imagine how relieved I was when a group of Oaklands students (Hollie, Katie and Rachael) accidentally stumbled across a formula for staging at least a starting point for such a scene.

> "Plays could possibly find some way into the 1990's by frankly being more theatrical. If theatre's going to exist, it has to be unashamedly theatrical and not rely on a fancy set, with a sofa and a French window."
>
> John Godber
> from www.johngodber.co.uk

After writing Too Much Punch I was often asked to run practical workshops for teachers and students on "how to stage a car accident". To do this I tried in vain to create such a formula using Essence Machines. I was convinced there was some kind of a link but never quite figured out where!

I explained how **Essence Machines** demonstrated a fractured approach to narrative similar to that which I used in writing my car accident scenes. These effectively helped to create a motif. I would then, as an entirely separate exercise, ask groups to create movement motifs for a moment in a car accident to offer a starting point (but never any more than a starting point) for a scene.

Groups who managed this difficult task would generally move on and apply their motif to produce imaginative work but there were no guarantees of success. It certainly wasn't a formula.

I fear, inadvertently, I set many groups up for failure. I would get away with it, as the workshops produced outstanding work from the most able. I was on the right lines but hadn't joined the dots.

I referred to these scenes and my workshops as **Human Pyrotechnics;** scenes where one would normally use pyrotechnics, but instead, use only the human body.

It took a group of my more daring students to join the dots for me. They did this purely as a challenge to themselves when my back was turned!

The Story Behind - Too Much Punch For Judy by Mark Wheeller

They went on to produce an Essence Machine of a car accident; teachers now refer to this as "scaffolding", to create an accident scene. Here's the recipe!

Motif:

* Groups of 4-7

* Select (or offer) an occupation as the stimulus. (E.g. secretary, teacher, shopkeeper)

* Groups choose a single phrase/statement typifying the occupation (stereotypes are fine/beneficial)

* The group then use one simple, brief movement to accompany the chosen line

* Practice until all in the group can present this as a choral/unison presentation with no individual differences… and bags of energy

* Motif provides a fast and easy way of depicting an occupational group

* John Godber uses this idea in both **Bouncers** & **Shakers**

* It is an effective way to enliven presentations and clarify narrative/character for the audience

* It can add humour and energy

* It provides clear evidence to an examiner that candidates have rehearsed

Motif leads naturally into the creation of:

Essence Machines:

Essence Machines encourage students to:

1. Select essential elements of scenes and cut the rubbish

2. Brainstorm a theme or revise content

3. Clarify the main points of Shakespeare (or any other play/story) plays

4. Re-cap a previous lesson (for absentee students or revision purposes)

The Story Behind - Too Much Punch For Judy by Mark Wheeller

Method:

* Groups of 4-7

* Group creates a Motif depicting the essence of a given title. (E.g. ***The Essence of a Summers Day*** – all say: "A Summers day!" accompanied by one simple gesture performed simultaneously. This becomes the opening of the Essence Machine

* Subsequently, one by one, each group member presents a solo line/simple movement (the rest of the group holding their still image). Each solo line/simple action should be a fragment of a typical moment from what might happen on a summer's day.
  The separate lines should not connect to other lines spoken by other people in the machine. (I.e. they should not be conversations).
  Each line/simple action will typify something someone might do or say given the starting point; e.g. "Can I have an ice-cream?" with a single action; in this instance, a hands together, praying motif under chin. This person then remains in this posture until the final choral line

* Each group member, in a pre-planned sequence (as unpredictable for the audience as possible), presents his or her fragmented line/action

* When the last group member completes his/her line/action, the whole group repeat their original motif (or a slight variant on it, where appropriate)

* The presentation ends with a freeze frame lasting approximately 5 seconds

Audience can "start" the machine by dropping a (mimed) coin into a (mimed) receptacle.

Essence Machines can be a great contribution for the Drama department/Youth Theatre group at a fete or Intake Evening.

Essence Machines are quick to prepare and look impressive when performed with energy.

Examples of essence machines:
Summer Holiday; Horror movie/Haunted House/Ghost train; School; Family life; Pre school television; War/Sci-Fi film; British Holiday; War; Xmas; Winter; Teenagers; Blokes on a night out (best performed by an all girl group); Ladettes on a night out (best performed by all boy group)

I have used the final two as an introduction to ***Bouncers/Shakers***.

The Story Behind - Too Much Punch For Judy by Mark Wheeller

Template for Car Accidents Essence Machines

First the group need to establish the circumstances of the accident. This can be the one from *Too Much Punch* (ignoring all in the words in the script but including the basic sequence of events).

I may, alternatively offer the outline of a scenario (in envelopes – enough for one per group) where appropriate. I have included four examples here for your use.

The point of this exercise is the staging rather than the creation of a story. The pre-prepared stories will hope to avoid lengthy discussions aimed at developing a plot.

Car Crash Scenario 1
(based on *Too Much Punch*)

* Two siblings go out for a night in the gym, or Zumba

* They are both drivers

* The last words from the mother before they left earlier that evening were "Be careful if you drink… get a taxi!"

* They decide to go to a wine bar after the gym/Zumba with friends

* There is a discussion between them about who should drive home (4 miles)

* It is decided that the sibling who does not own the car should drive because he/she is less drunk… and does not have a drink drive case pending

* On the way home they crash into a small bridge at the side of the road built with scaffolding poles

* A man in a nearby house is woken up by the bang and comes out to try and help. He finds the passenger is dead and tries to move the driver away

* The driver is uninjured

* The passenger is decapitated by one of the scaffolding bars on the bridge

* The police are called

* They tell the mother who is very upset

* Life goes on. The one who has killed has to live with the guilt of the killing and has many nightmares about it afterwards

The Story Behind - Too Much Punch For Judy by Mark Wheeller

Car Crash Scenario 2

* A young person is having his/her first driving lesson
* Parents provided these lessons for a recent birthday present
* The young person had been excited by the prospect of driving lessons
* A small child asks mum or dad for money to buy an ice cream
* Money is given to the child who crosses the road to buy the ice cream
* Ice cream is bought
* Child rushes back across the road without looking
* Child runs into an oncoming car
* The parents of the victim child are informed
* The parents of the learner driver are informed
* Life will never be the same

The Story Behind - Too Much Punch For Judy by Mark Wheeller

Car Crash Scenario 3
(Based on *Legal Weapon*) by Mark Wheeller

* A girl says goodbye to her mum

* She is riding to a job interview on her new moped

* She stops to get some petrol

* A man is on his way to work. His girlfriend has just moved away to Uni. He was talking to her on Face book. This made him late for an important appointment. He is speeding

* The girl leaves the petrol station

* The man is travelling towards her and doesn't have time to stop

* He swerves

* He hits the motorbike

* She is thrown off and killed instantly

* Her mum is informed

* He makes a phone call to his girlfriend who is away at Uni

* He is arrested

Page to Stage

The Story Behind - Too Much Punch For Judy by Mark Wheeller

Car Crash Scenario 4
(Inspired by *Chicken*) by Mark Wheeller

* Two boys are walking home from school

* They decide to play chicken on the road

* One dares the other to cross the road as late as possible in front of an oncoming car

* The first films the dare on his mobile

* Meanwhile a girl is driving her school children home from Primary school

* Her children are arguing in the back of the car

* She turns to tell them off and crashes into the boy playing chicken

Page to Stage

The Story Behind - Too Much Punch For Judy by Mark Wheeller

Method:

* Opening motif – **the moment of impact.**
  This needs to be "represented" (not an imitation of reality) by the whole group in a high-energy manner. Physicalise the violence of the moment safely. This selected "moment" will start the second before the impact and end the moment after it. It is one simple movement. The simple movement is accompanied by one simple line – often "No!!!" Victim, perpetrator and observers can also say a line such as this. It must be a BRIEF movement and line.

* This "moment" will be followed by one full round of solo lines from each group member to build up the narrative of the accident. It will show fragments of the events leading up to the accident.
  These events could be in the moments immediately before the crash or much further in the back-story.

* A second round of solo lines follow to show the aftermath of the accident. These are again performed as fragmented single lines/simple actions

* The Car Accident Essence Machine closes with a high-energy reprise of the moment of impact, or a slight variant, where appropriate

I reduce this to the following for a student hand out.

1. Moment of impact: word/short phrase; possibly "NO!" or "Look out!"
2. Each person performs one line/movement - before the accident
3. Each person performs one line/movement - after the accident.
4. The moment of impact is re-performed, perhaps a variant?

Once this has been developed groups will generate a number of ideas, which can be applied to any given car accident.

Page to Stage

The Story Behind - Too Much Punch For Judy by Mark Wheeller

I used this technique to initiate a group in OYT who were working towards a performance on a DVD[35] aiming to demonstrate the staging of Wheellerplays.

This group, an experienced group of 18 year olds who had been in OYT for up to five years, wanted to take on the challenge of creating the crash scene from *Too Much Punch*.

I added one further idea: that they use scaffolding poles from our lighting tower. I selected these, as that was the material Jo's car actually crashed into.

This group had never before attempted to stage an accident scene, nor seen the play in performance.
The group included my son, Charlie, who had, at Sixth Form College, developed a passion for Physical Theatre and Dance. He took the lead and directed the scene as he gradually developed a vision of how it could be.

Charlie takes up the story of how they created their version of this scene.

> *"I took the opportunity to throw a new slant onto this scene, adding more physicality. The integral nature of using set and props interested me to create new and exciting concept. My dad wanted us to use huge scaffolding bars. With such great potential we started throwing paint at the blank page we had.*
> *I had no idea what the end product would look like, but I knew I wanted it to be high energy, lots of twisting, tangling and maximum noise. We explored different ways of moving around the scaffolding bars but were determined to remain true to the real life incident. We brought in a musician to write an original underscore to help create the atmosphere. After listening to the soundtrack I started to see intertwining lifts and jumps and a range of ways of using the metal poles. We pieced our ideas together and the scene was complete. Looking back on it I would love to have more time to explore the scene further and ultimately, see if the whole play could be redirected around the feel of what we did."*
>
> **Charlie Wheeller 2012.**

They used music, movement and multimedia to great effect and if you haven't seen it, do get the DVD. It is worth it for this scene alone. It provides a model of a group of young people finding untapped potential in a scene.

It stands for me as the best *Too Much Punch* accident scene I have seen.

---

*(35) **The Definitive Authors Collection** scripts are published by www.zincpublishing.co.uk and the staged versions are on dvd from Wheellerplays@gmail.com*

The Story Behind - Too Much Punch For Judy by Mark Wheeller

Afterthought: - Too Much Punch For Judy: Re-visitation

Writing this book has brought *Too Much Punch For Judy* from 1987 forward into my present after being absent for a long while. It has unexpectedly inspired me to mount a new version, which I will present with Oasis Youth Theatre in Southampton in March 2013. This will offer me an opportunity to incorporate ideas I have seen and benefit from the experience gained over the years to create a fresh 25th anniversary production.

We intend to film this production for a DVD that will be made available… finally! [36]

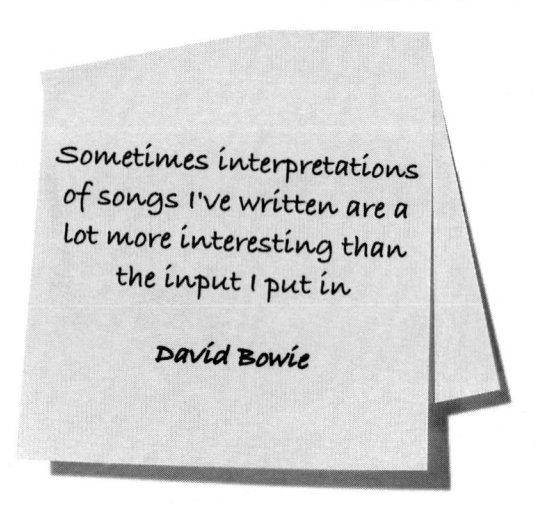

Sometimes interpretations of songs I've written are a lot more interesting than the input I put in

David Bowie

As a playwright I have been exceptionally lucky over the years to see professional productions of six of my plays offering me, new and exciting ways of seeing them. It is however seeing a school production of *Graham – World's Fastest Blind Runner* that most influenced my directorial approach and has in turn, initiated a run of incredible success with OYT, which I hope this production of *Too Much Punch* will build upon.

In the summer of 2007 I received an invitation from Catherine Hudson, a drama teacher at Therfield School (Leatherhead), to see her production of *Graham – World's Fastest Blind Runner*, which had won a local Amateur Drama Festival qualifying it for the *National Drama Festivals Association (NDFA), England Winners Festival*. Among those to be in the audience was Sir Michael Caine. I had already decided to mount my own production of that play the following year and thought it may well be useful to see another interpretation of it, particularly one that had achieved some, albeit limited, critical acclaim.

It was original and differently staged to anything I could ever have conceived. It had a clear directorial "vision", with the large cast costumed in black with white gloves (and Graham in white). Each performer had a white cane, which was used in different, imaginative ways throughout the play. They also had specially commissioned music. I was knocked out by its vision and it extended my thinking about the play… in fact my plays.

---

[36] *The dvd of this production of Too Much Punch For Judy is now available from Wheellerplays@gmail.com.*

The Story Behind - Too Much Punch For Judy by Mark Wheeller

The Therfield production of *Graham* won the *All Winners Festival* and went on to represent England in the *NDFA British Final*.

Unlike the Therfield production, mine prior to that tended to use small casts (2m 2f), partly to road test them for professional use. I felt, with these small casts we could match the quality of the professionals. The Therfield produc-tion was refreshing using an onstage chorus throughout; an approach no small-scale professional Theatre Company could ever match, as it would be so expensive to employ the performers! Consequently their production achieved something small professional companies could never match!

I decided to use Catherine's ideas as a starting point for my OYT production of *Graham.* It was a bigger success than I could ever have imagined. We went on to become the first group from our region to reach the English Final of the All England Theatre Festival, (the rival festival to the NDFA). I had been entering AETF's for over 25 years and my productions had never progressed beyond the first round! [37]

The following year we presented **One Million to STOP THE TRAFFIK** and had a cast of 18, purely because that's how many wanted to be involved. I imagined a few would drop out but they didn't! I wrote it with a cast of six in mind but felt bad kicking 12 out. I applied Catherine's chorus idea and, with the cast, created a far more imaginative interpretation that I am very proud of. We went on to win the AETF English Final leading us to represent England in the **British Final of One-Act Plays.** [38]

Between 2010-2012 I worked with OYT on a version of **Jack** (and the Beanstalk), performing a free adaptation with puppetry and no recognisable language using a "Hudson" chorus to make the story telling more imaginative. This also won through to the *AETF English Final* (winning the *Rex Walford Award for "Creativity"*). A hat-trick of OYT productions to reach the *English Final*! [39]

I also commissioned a musical underscore for each of these productions, adding invaluable atmosphere to the final performance.

The 25th anniversary production of **Too Much Punch For Judy** had a "Hudson/Therfield" chorus and an original underscore composed by Paul Ibbott, Head of Performing Arts at our Oasis Academy in Southampton. Inspired by **London Road**, I have also wrote two songs lyrics using testimony, to provide Paul with a stimulus for the underscored musical themes. One of these songs was used in the final production.

---

(37) *Graham - World's Fastest Blind Runner - as performed by OYT is published by www.zincpublishing.co.uk, and the staged versions are on the dvd from Wheellerplays@gmail.com*
(38) *One Million to STOP THE TRAFFIK as performed by OYT is published by www.zincpublishing.co.uk, and the staged versions are on the dvd from Wheellerplays@gmail.com*
(39) *Jack is published by www.resources4drama.co.uk, and the staged versions are also available on the dvd*

The Story Behind - Too Much Punch For Judy by Mark Wheeller

I also wrote a new Prologue to replace the existing Epilogue. This gave the play a different focus from thoughts writing this book has highlighted and also in an attempt to deal with a criticism of being "finger wagging" and didactic, often made of my work. I don't apologise for this, as I believe passionately in the subjects I write about. However, there are those who suggest that this "finger-wagging" can be off putting. I was keen to find a way to re-frame this, openly propagandist, play. I hope I have done this using a simple question:

Can an openly propagandist play such as this have any hope of being successful in changing hearts and minds, when the person who committed the offence went on to commit it again ?

The Story Behind - Too Much Punch For Judy by Mark Wheeller

I took the opportunity to integrate the physical theatre feel of Charlie's accident scene into the whole play, as my Charlie wanted to do. As a graduate from The National Centre for Circus Arts he said to me that he wants to fuse circus skills into some of my plays. I await his first attempt at this with eager anticipation!

The 25th anniversary production provided a great opportunity to assemble many of those, amateur and professional, who have been involved with this play over the last 25 years. We were fortunate to include interviews with Fay Davies, Matt Allen and Charlie Wheeller amongst others as bonus bits on the dvd.

Finally, we hope it can continue to highlight the drink and drug driving as an on-going issue for its time.

No matter what I go on to achieve later on in my career, I predict that the play likely to remain most closely associated with Mark Wheeller will be… *Too Much Punch For Judy.* I am very happy about that.

Oasis Youth Theatre rehearsing for the 25th anniversary production of *Too Much Punch For Judy*.

The Story Behind - Too Much Punch For Judy by Mark Wheeller

Appendix 2: - Essex Police Accident Photographs

May 20th 1983:
A lonely road near Epping. A Renault 5 car comes off the road and hits a bridge. The scaffolding construction slices through the car windscreen. The driver, Judy, escapes unhurt but the passenger, her sister Joanna, is killed outright. Jo and Judy had both been drinking.

The Story Behind - Too Much Punch For Judy by Mark Wheeller

The Story Behind - Too Much Punch For Judy by Mark Wheeller

The Story Behind - Too Much Punch For Judy by Mark Wheeller

Second edition postscript: - Too Much Punch For Judy

Since the publication of this book, Too Much Punch's life has continued. It nearly became a set text on one of the GCSE 9-1 course specifications but was pulled because, at that point in time, the whole script didn't appear in one book. The opening, developed for the 25th anniversary production, only appeared as an appendix in the first edition of this book until, last year, a new edition of the play-text was released. Now the script is all in one edition I am hopeful it will be reconsidered. It is amazing that these plays originating from my humble unfunded Youth Theatre groups are considered so seriously. I could never have imagined this when I started out. It seems unreal… but it is heart-warming to have the interest this kind of coverage generates… not to mention the book sales and workshop bookings!

In 2016 Too Much Punch also achieved the landmark of having 6,000 licensed performances. This seems unbelievable but it is true. I have been fastidious in my record keeping. I am so glad I went to see the performance. At one point I wasn't going to and then I heard from my daughter, Daisy, that her friend, Scott had been cast as Bob and Chris Caten.

Almost immediately I decided to go and I booked my flight to Jersey (who have had presented a professional tour every year for the past 20!) I remember thinking that I doubt I would be alive for the 7,000th so I couldn't believe I had originally thought I would miss it. The other intriguing factor was that Michelle Smith, one of the founding members of the Paper Birds was directing it. I'm glad I did go. The performance was great and really didn't seem to have dated. Two girls ran out crying and shouting. Many more were crying more quietly. Its power certainly remained.

At lunchtime, I spoke with the cast and tipped them off about the upcoming I Love You Mum – I Promise I Won't Die auditions the next week. Ben O'Shea was particularly enthusiastic and arranged to attend. He was cast as Jack.

The Story Behind - Too Much Punch For Judy by Mark Wheeller

I was introduced to verbatim theatre and Mark Wheeller's work when I was in secondary school. We studied a few of his texts and I saw the Ape Theatre production in our school hall. It made us laugh and then shook us to our core. The comedy was important as it created light and shade in an otherwise downbeat story. The characters are heightened yet relatable, as we forge a relationship with them, becoming emotionally involved as the plot reveals the horrific true fate of its drink driver, and her sister. We must realise that these people were just like us… youths looking for a good time that made a mistake. It had a profound effect on me and, thirteen years on, I remember it vividly. I am living (emphasis on living) proof that 'Too Much Punch For Judy' is a powerful, educational tool.

In 2016 I was in Love Theatre's tour of secondary schools in Jersey, from where I originate. My experience and advice to performers is to break the fourth wall at every opportunity. Send the message directly into the eyes of your audience from start to finish. We had many students crying and a couple having to leave the theatre. Feedback after performances further confirmed the effect of this play.

My involvement will remain a special memory for me for many reasons:

* I was able to work with director Michelle Smith, who had taught me A-level Performing Arts and supported me on my journey to university to study acting. Her theatrical vision is simple, unpretentious, accessible and effective. We had a wonderfully playful and efficient rehearsal process. She introduced each performance, establishing the words were taken from interviews with the real people. This was genius and instantly drew out an energy and focus in a teenage audience who were sat in their school hall so early in the morning. I watched every day with awe at the effect the play was having.

* I used my skills as a performer to educate students from my home-town.
* One of our performances was the 6,000th!
* We met Mark who became the link between the reality of the tale and our theatrical interpretation. He was also an eager listener, curious about our experiences of his work and the effect it was having on audiences.

The Story Behind - Too Much Punch For Judy by Mark Wheeller

There is a stigma against Theatre in Education (T.I.E) stemming from weak companies or performances, dumbing down theatre for young audiences. If you only provide a simple storyline or worse, artificial acting, you will lose them in the first couple of minutes. Mark's plays have countered this approach for years, providing painfully truthful experiences combined with performances that use infinite inventiveness, connect to audiences and do change lives. Mark's work has eliminated the stigma and has challenged me as a performer in many ways. I am very grateful for the life/career experience and now have a far greater respect for TIE/verbatim theatre.

Ben O'Shea

The Story Behind - Too Much Punch For Judy by Mark Wheeller

I remember talking to the cast over lunch between their performances about a line in the play which has since been pointed out to me as hugely significant... and to be honest I'd never really considered it. Chris Caten says a seemingly innocuous line on page 27 of the new edition of the scrip

Chris: As we made our way towards Epping, I happened to note Jo and Judy drive by. I'd known their family for... well over ten years. I supposed they'd been out enjoying themselves.

Matt, the Ape director, during one of his workshops with my OYT cast, pointed out that if Chris had "known" Jo and Judy that well he would have known exactly what "enjoying themselves" meant. Perhaps he felt some guilt at not following up that thought? This puts a quite different spin the psychology of his actions. I found it fascinating that I had not even considered this potential subtext previously. There is always something new to learn about the play... even for me!

Page to Stage

Bob and Nob went down surprisingly well. I've sometimes described it as a "poor-man's Godber" scene. I have never had much confidence in it. Bearing this in mind, you can imagine my surprise when, earlier that year, in Covent Garden Market, I was buying something with my credit card and, noticing my name, the trader asked if I was "the Mark Wheeller". On discovering I was, he launched into a recitation of the Bob and Nob lines, just as I might have done with the Parrot Sketch as a teenage Monty Python fan. He knew it word for word, remembering it from his GCSE exam. It was one of the best spontaneous tributes I've ever received... though I was a bit embarrassed!

I have always had a fear that the Nurse scene loses pace. In Love Theatre's version it didn't. The actors were exceptional. I remember thinking how fortunate I am to have seen my work be interpreted by a range of professionals so frequently! As always I was interested to see different approaches to scenes and Caten's revelation to Judy in the hospital was presented successfully in a completely different way to the one I was used to. Despite it not being accurate, it added freshness and "worked" wonderfully! It brought opportunities of a more emotional approach to the scene. One criticism of my own approach to my plays is that they have a "British reserve" with regards to emotions. They work even better when this is removed and in my current production of **Butcher, Butcher Burning Bright** with RSCoYT I am really trying to overcome this possible weakness. An interesting development to note!

The Story Behind - Too Much Punch For Judy by Mark Wheeller

The other "first" the play experienced was a professional performance in London at the Camden Fringe. It had a full cast who were cast age correctly which I'd only seen once before.

I loved it and wrote this review on my Wheellerplays Facebook page. Any potential directors will be fascinated to see the idea Alex Cobb had as director to bring new life to the accident scene (amongst other things).

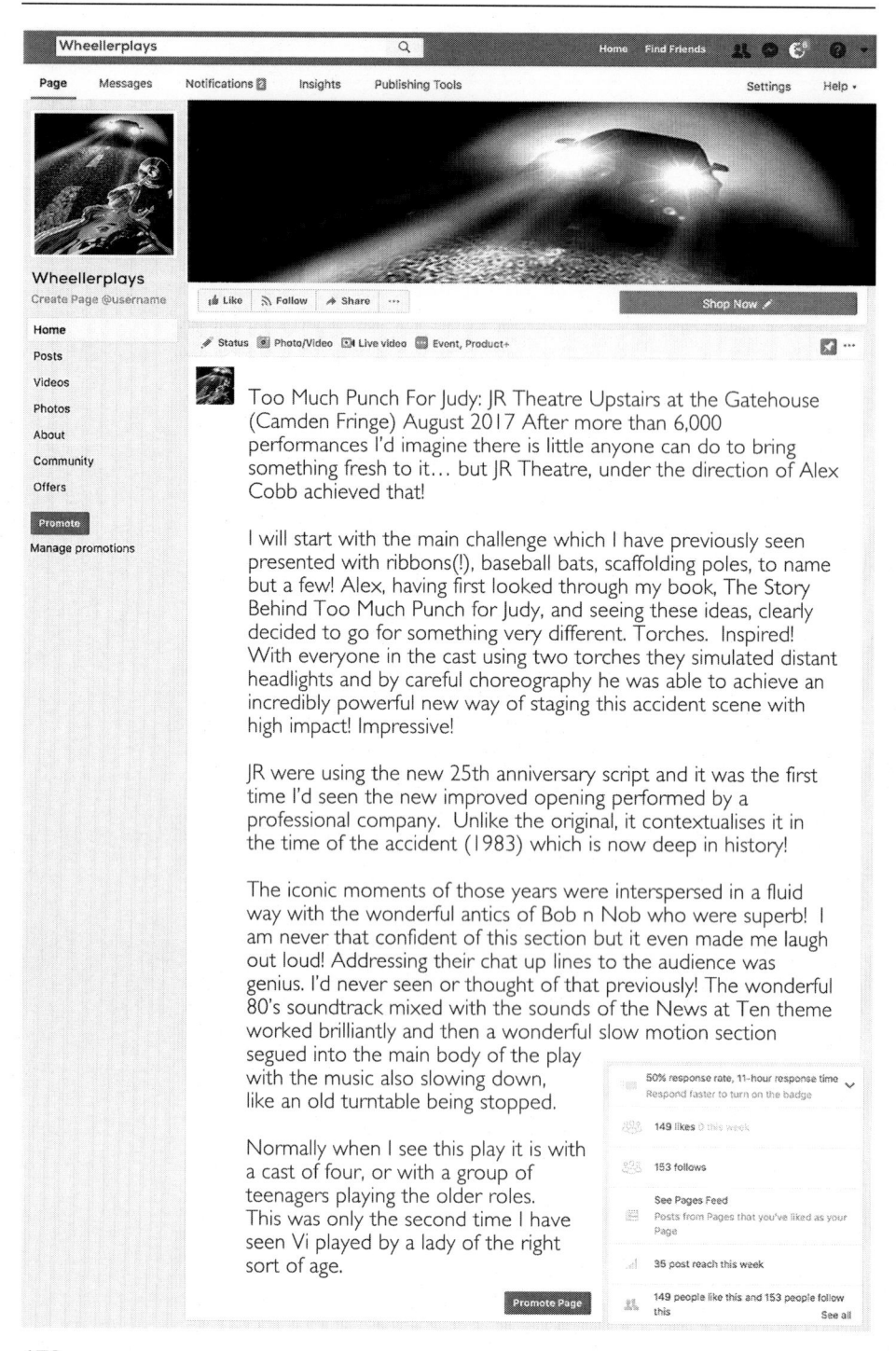

The Story Behind - Too Much Punch For Judy by Mark Wheeller

Too Much Punch For Judy: JR Theatre Upstairs at the Gatehouse (Camden Fringe) August 2017 After more than 6,000 performances I'd imagine there is little anyone can do to bring something fresh to it… but JR Theatre, under the direction of Alex Cobb achieved that!

I will start with the main challenge which I have previously seen presented with ribbons(!), baseball bats, scaffolding poles, to name but a few! Alex, having first looked through my book, The Story Behind Too Much Punch for Judy, and seeing these ideas, clearly decided to go for something very different. Torches. Inspired! With everyone in the cast using two torches they simulated distant headlights and by careful choreography he was able to achieve an incredibly powerful new way of staging this accident scene with high impact! Impressive!

JR were using the new 25th anniversary script and it was the first time I'd seen the new improved opening performed by a professional company. Unlike the original, it contextualises it in the time of the accident (1983) which is now deep in history!

The iconic moments of those years were interspersed in a fluid way with the wonderful antics of Bob n Nob who were superb! I am never that confident of this section but it even made me laugh out loud! Addressing their chat up lines to the audience was genius. I'd never seen or thought of that previously! The wonderful 80's soundtrack mixed with the sounds of the News at Ten theme worked brilliantly and then a wonderful slow motion section segued into the main body of the play with the music also slowing down, like an old turntable being stopped.

Normally when I see this play it is with a cast of four, or with a group of teenagers playing the older roles. This was only the second time I have seen Vi played by a lady of the right sort of age.

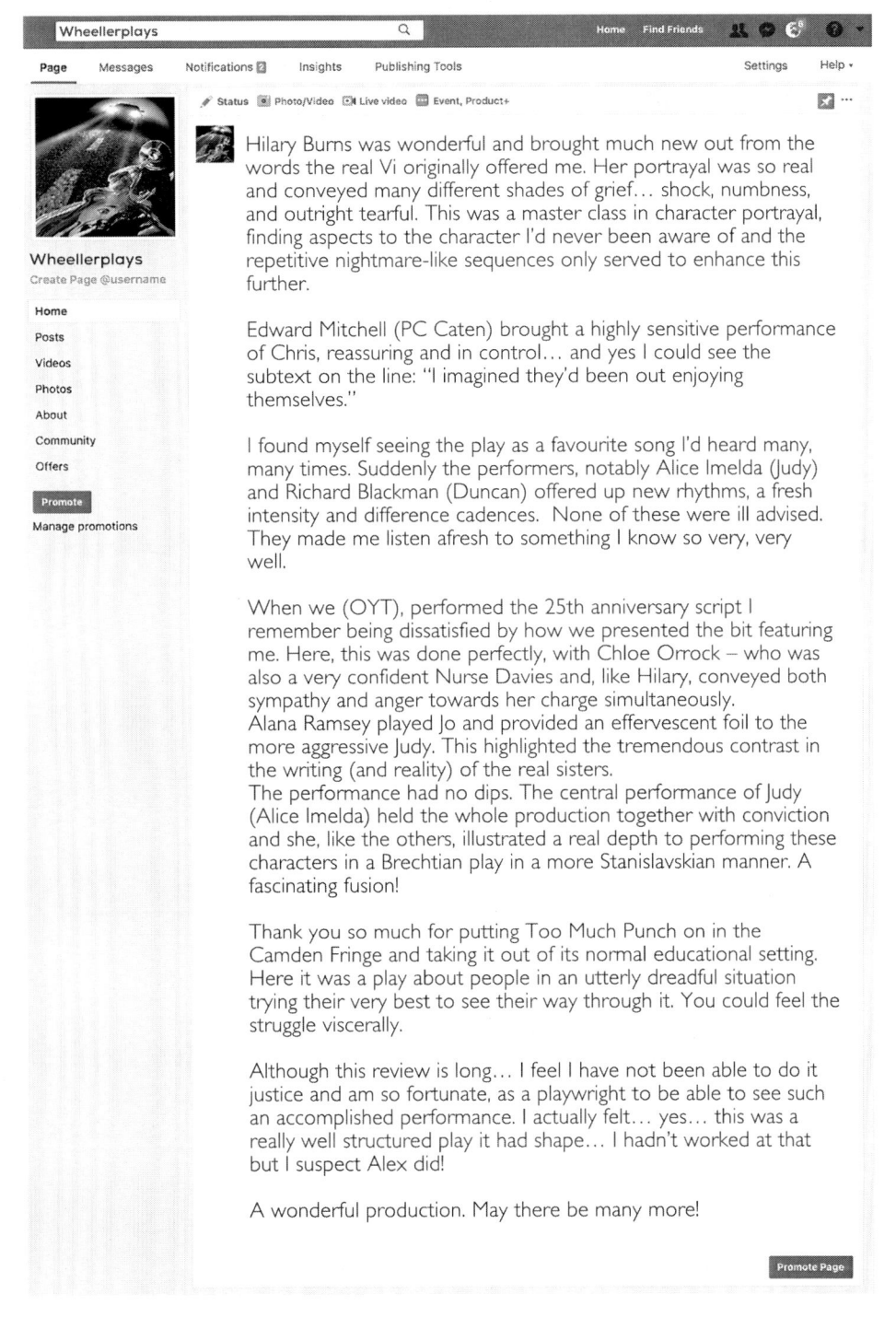

The Story Behind - Too Much Punch For Judy by Mark Wheeller

Hilary Burns was wonderful and brought much new out from the words the real Vi originally offered me. Her portrayal was so real and conveyed many different shades of grief… shock, numbness, and outright tearful. This was a master class in character portrayal, finding aspects to the character I'd never been aware of and the repetitive nightmare-like sequences only served to enhance this further.

Edward Mitchell (PC Caten) brought a highly sensitive performance of Chris, reassuring and in control… and yes I could see the subtext on the line: "I imagined they'd been out enjoying themselves."

I found myself seeing the play as a favourite song I'd heard many, many times. Suddenly the performers, notably Alice Imelda (Judy) and Richard Blackman (Duncan) offered up new rhythms, a fresh intensity and difference cadences. None of these were ill advised. They made me listen afresh to something I know so very, very well.

When we (OYT), performed the 25th anniversary script I remember being dissatisfied by how we presented the bit featuring me. Here, this was done perfectly, with Chloe Orrock – who was also a very confident Nurse Davies and, like Hilary, conveyed both sympathy and anger towards her charge simultaneously.
Alana Ramsey played Jo and provided an effervescent foil to the more aggressive Judy. This highlighted the tremendous contrast in the writing (and reality) of the real sisters.
The performance had no dips. The central performance of Judy (Alice Imelda) held the whole production together with conviction and she, like the others, illustrated a real depth to performing these characters in a Brechtian play in a more Stanislavskian manner. A fascinating fusion!

Thank you so much for putting Too Much Punch on in the Camden Fringe and taking it out of its normal educational setting. Here it was a play about people in an utterly dreadful situation trying their very best to see their way through it. You could feel the struggle viscerally.

Although this review is long… I feel I have not been able to do it justice and am so fortunate, as a playwright to be able to see such an accomplished performance. I actually felt… yes… this was a really well structured play it had shape… I hadn't worked at that but I suspect Alex did!

A wonderful production. May there be many more!

The Story Behind - Too Much Punch For Judy by Mark Wheeller

I think it is fitting, as a final page, to include a picture of (and a quote from) Fay Davies our Judy from 1987 and Alice Imelda, the Judy from 2017, when they met up at the JR production in Camden (2017) 30 years after Fay premiered the play in our little Epping St John's School Drama Studio.

It means so much to me that the cast like to keep up with the adventures of my little play all these years later. It really was a special group of (now not so) young people who gave so much of their time to develop this unique production that has gone on to exceeded any hopes and ambitions I could ever have had for it!

> What a gripping performance! There were changes I'd not seen before. It was the first time I'd seen it presented by professionals where each role was played by a separate performer. The music from the period set it perfectly. It was just as explosive, compelling and real as it was for me as fourteen year old, 30 years ago. It hadn't lost anything and seems to have matured with time. People were in floods of tears... even my boyfriend cried! It was an amazing production. It seems to have become an important piece of drink drive history.
>
> Fay Davies

The Story Behind - Too Much Punch For Judy by Mark Wheeller

Bibliography:
Esslin, Martin. A Choice of Evils. (London: Eyre Methuen, 1959) Hewitt, Paulo & Weller, John. Steve Marriott - All Too Beautiful... (London: Helter Skelter Publishing 2004) Wheeller, Mark. Too Much Punch For Judy. (London IAS 1987 & London: dbda 1999 2013 Ten Alps, now Zinc Publishing) Legal Weapon. (London: dbda 1999 now Zinc Publishing)

Newspaper
Amateur Stage
Epping Star
The Guardian
News of the World
The Scotsman
The Sun
Times Educational Supplement
The Wellington Evening Post
West Essex Gazette,

Quotes:
Bush, Kate. Advice to Young Songwriters. Classic Rock Magazine 2011
Bowie, David. Rock's Heathen Speaks. 2002 http://www.concertlivewire.com/interviews/bowie.htm
Godber, John. www.johngodber.co.uk
Horn, Goldie. Let Go And Trust. http://www.mindbodygreen.com/0-3029/Goldie-Hawn-Let-Go-and-Trust.html Jobs, Steve. One Last Thing. PBS, 1994
Nevitt, Roy. Living Archive Project, 1982. http://www.livingarchive.org.uk
Plath, Sylvia. The Journals of Sylvia Plath, Smith College 1950-1955.
Shankula, Henry. Review of Too Much Punch For Judy. Addiction Research Foundation. Toronto 1988.
Ohono, Taiichi. Do Not Fear Failure. http://www.shmula.com/taiichi-ohno-do-not-fear-failure/9290/

The Story Behind - Too Much Punch For Judy by Mark Wheeller

About the Author:
Mark has written plays and musicals since his schooldays at Marlwood School, Bristol. No rock bands would play his songs so he wrote musicals to get them performed! Most remain unknown but his plays went on to achieve success. **Too Much Punch for Judy** (1987) is one of the most performed contemporary plays in the world having been performed over 6000 times in its short life. **Hard To Swallow** and **Missing Dan Nolan** are both set texts for the 9-1 GCSE (Eduqas & OCR respectively) specifications. His works are used extensively in schools across the world. He retired after 36 years of teaching, which was charted in his popular 2010 book **Drama Schemes** (Rhinegold) and **The Drama Club** (Pping). A teachers resource book on **Hard to Swallow (Hard to Swallow – Easy To Digest)** was published in 2017.

His most recent commissions (2015/6) were: **Scratching the Surface** (Pping) and **I Love You, Mum – I Promise I Won't Die** (Methuen). **I Love You Mum**, as performed by Stopwatch Theatre Company, toured schools from 2017. His plays are becoming increasingly popular as they feature on DVD.

Mark lives with his wife, Rachael in Southampton where he works part-time as the Director of Romsey School Community Youth Theatre (RSCoYT). He runs workshops on his plays all over the world.

The Story Behind - Too Much Punch For Judy by Mark Wheeller

Barrie Sapsford

When Mark asked me to help him with this project, I was truly honored. We have been friends for over 35 years now, despite starting out as my drama teacher, he had an amazing way of connecting with his students and seeing the best in them. I wouldn't be where I am today without his influence. At school, I was that troubled child who spoke with his fists. My frustrations had no outlet and the need for attention was only ever satisfied by long lectures from the headmaster for my un-welcomed actions towards fellow students. I loved music and drama and Mark recognised that he could channel this angry teenager's frustration and passion into more creative and productive activities that would be rewarding as well as distracting enough to keep me out of trouble. I lapped up the adulation with every performance and suddenly, I was popular, this time for all the right reasons!

My parents, teachers and classmates all saw a different side to me, a side that I was becoming immensely proud of. EYT gave me confidence; the fun of being on stage and performing in theatres all over the UK is an experience that set the foundation for everything I have achieved since. I have addressed hundreds of people in conferences, presentations and meetings in my many careers, hosted charity events and fund raisers in top London hotels to church fates, all because of the skills I learned through drama and acting. I think back to when I left school but was still involved in Epping Youth Theatre (EYT). I secured my first job in an Art & Printing company because I was in EYT. They had done the artwork and poster printing for **Race to be Seen**, and the company owner loved Am-Dram.

There is so much I could say and stories I could tell about being part of TMPFJ, which could add a whole new chapter to this book(!) but it's not about me. I have so many fond memories. I love the fact that groups of us meet up from time to time for a BBQ or to see a show. Our friendships have withstood the test of time. One thing that has stuck with me and has become something of a philosophy of mine helping me build my businesses, is something Mark shared with me when I left school. I asked him *why did he think he became so popular with students*. When he started at my school, only 15 of us took drama as a subject, by the following year they had to employ additional teachers to cope with demand! I worked out for myself that he was easy to get along with and some of his popularity was down to the fact that he allowed us to call him by his first name, (a very bold move in my school), but what I didn't understand was the psychology behind it. He said:
"I believe in making friends. If I ask a student to do something, I am often met with resistance, however, if I am considered as their friend, I get the opposite reaction, as most people will do anything for a friend, without question".

This was a great life lesson, if only all teachers and bosses thought this way.

The Story Behind - Too Much Punch For Judy by Mark Wheeller

Other publications by Mark Wheeller:

Plays
Graham - Worlds Fastest Blind Runner! (Zinc Publishing)
Too Much Punch For Judy (Zinc Publishing)
Hard To Swallow (Zinc Publishing)
Chicken! (Zinc Publishing)
Sweet FA (SchoolPlay Productions)
Chunnel Of Love (Zig Zag)
Legal Weapon & II (Zinc Publishings)
Butcher, Butcher Burning Bright (formerly Arson About) (Oxford University Press)
The Gate Escape (Zinc Publishing)
Missing Dan Nolan (Zinc Publishing)
Sequinned Suits and Platform Boots/(We Were) Ziggy's Band (Resources4drama)
Jamie in The Land of Dinnersphere (Zinc Publishing)
Kill Jill (Zinc Publishing)
Granny and the Wolf (Pearson/Longman)
Driven to Distraction (Zinc Publishing)
One Million to STOP THE TRAFFIK (Zinc Publishing)
The Wheeler Deal - 3 Short Plays, Damon & Bazza Lads, Always in a Hurry & Parents! (Resources4drama) Wheellerplays – The Author's Definitive Collection (A Collection of Wheellerscenes) (Zinc Publishing)
Jack (Resources4Drama)
Chequered Flags to Chequered Futures (Zinc Publishing)
Scratching the Surface (Pping)
I Love You, Mum I Promise I Won't Die (Methuen)
Crossing the Bridge – The Unseen Billy Goats Scenes from Hard to Swallow (Resources4Drama)
This is For You (Pping Publishing)
Can You Hear Me Major Tom? (Pping Publishing)

Musicals
King Arthur - All Shook Up. (SchoolPlay Productions)
Blackout (SchoolPlay Productions)
No Place For A Girl (SchoolPlay Productions)
The Most Absurd Xmas Musical In The World… Ever! (SchoolPlay Productions)
Wacky Soap (Zinc Publishing)

The Story Behind - Too Much Punch For Judy by Mark Wheeller

Other publications by Mark Wheeller: *cont.*

Productions on YouTube
Blackout – Operation Pied Piper
Wacky Soap

DVD's
Available from: wheellerplays@gmail.com

Wheellerplays Exemplified
Graham - Worlds Fastest Blindman!
Wheellerplays – The Definitive Collection
One Million To STOP THE TRAFFIK Too Much Punch For Judy
Jack (Physical Theatre – no recognisable words)
Chequered Futures to Chequered Flags/Chicken (Double bill)
Bang Out Of Order by Johnny Carrington & Danny Sturrock.
Missing Dan Nolan
Scratching the Surface
I Love You, Mum – I Promise I Won't Die
Hard To Swallow

Graham - Worlds Fastest Blindman

DVD's of Mark's work now available from Pping Publishing at *www.wheellerplays.com* or email *Wheellerplays@gmail.com*

Books
Tufty's Adventures (RoSPA)
Wacky Soap Storybook (Zinc Publications)
Drama Schemes (Rhinegold)
The Drama Club (Pping/Resources4Drama)
Hard to Swallow – Easy to Digest (Tbc)

Missing Dan Nolan

I Love You, Mum – I Promise I Won't Die

Jack - Physical Theatre

180

The Story Behind - Too Much Punch For Judy by Mark Wheeller

Scratching the Surface (Pping Publishing)

Scratching the Surface is now available from Mark Wheeller *(wheellerplays@gmail.com)* as a script and as a DVD.

"It is important that everyone feels able to talk about mental health issues - they affect one in four of us - and plays like the excellent, "Scratching the Surface", are really important in giving mental health, particularly in how it affects younger people, the attention it deserves and needs."
Solihull MIND

This new verbatim play by Mark Wheeller dramatises the story of his interviews with Rob, a young man who, as a teenager, self-harmed. Mark chats to his family as they reflect on the trauma of living with this constant "elephant in the room", as they describe it. Mark then went on to talk with a group of randomly selected students from a school in the Midlands. This encounter was equally shocking as gradually all of them admitted they had either encountered someone who had self harmed or had themselves self harmed. One thirteen year old described it as "the mouse in the room"

"You feel like a small helpless being, to the point that you'd hurt yourself and everyone around is different to you."

"Great play that my students have really engaged with. I've never had Year 9 ask to keep reading a play rather than getting up to do practical. They found it fascinating and said they thought it was great the way the play used the teenagers own words. Really recommend to anyone working in a high school."
Amazon Verified buyer review.

A Verbatim Play by

Mark Wheeller

Commissioned by Alderbrook School

The Story Behind - Too Much Punch For Judy by Mark Wheeller

The Drama Club (Pping Publishing)

The Drama Club is now available from Mark Wheeller *(wheellerplays@gmail.com)* or Clive Hulme
(www.resources4drama.co.uk) as a book with plenty of downloads!

This is the record of a project which Mark Wheeller never wanted to be involved in - a Junior School Drama Club - but which resulted in a triumph. Mark takes us through the process of what happened step by step and gives practical advice on running a similar project in your own school or club. The book includes a 10 scene, multi-actor script and access to an online support pack from Resources4Drama. This is an ideal source book for those looking for inspiration to run their own extra curricular Drama activities with children and young people. The innovative guide guarantees parental involvement and appreciation.

"I must admit that when I first opened the package my heart sank, I was hoping for something a little....bigger. Nevertheless, in the old adage of don't judge a book by its cover (or its size) I gave it a read. I have taught drama for over 20 years and although I love my subject, can often get stuck in a rut. This book gave me a different perspective on how to approach drama with this age range. I was really impressed with some of the new ideas and at their simplicity too".

Not only are the ideas there but a 10 scene script that you can start putting into practice immediately. My drama class will be working with and adapting Midnight to suit them this term.... I really am excited about trying out some of the projects in this book and would wholeheartedly recommend. Concluding that size really doesn't matter after all!

"Well done Mark Wheeller and Clive Hulme on creating a really different drama book worth every penny."
Amazon Verified Reviewer.

The Story Behind - Too Much Punch For Judy by Mark Wheeller

Hard to Swallow – Easy to Digest (Pping Publishing)

Hard to Swallow – Easy to Digest is now available from Mark Wheeller (**wheellerplays@gmail.com**) and Karen Latto (**www.karenlatto.com**). The official DVD performance is also available to buy, performed by students from The Romsey School

Hard to Swallow is an adaptation of Maureen Dunbar's award winning book/film Catherine. It charts her daughter's uneven battle with anorexia and her family's difficulty in coping with it. It was premiered at the Edinburgh Festival Fringe in 1989 and, the following year was invited to be performed at the Royal National Theatre on the world famous Olivier stage. Hard to Swallow has been performed across the world achieving popularity in both schools and One Act Drama Festivals. In 2016 it was selected as one of the set texts for Eduqas' new GCSE Drama 9-1 specification.

Students are now expected to study the way Hard to Swallow was developed and presented. This fascinating story has now been uncovered. Mark's book uses vivid reminiscences of his Oaklands Youth Theatre cast to describe the development of the play and those early performances.

Hard to Swallow – Easy To Digest
Mark Wheeller
Scheme of Work by Karen Latto

Adrian New goes on to reveal StopWatch Theatre Company's professional tour which followed in 1990. Karen Latto a former Exam Board Subject Specialist has added an invaluable scheme of work to be used by teachers who teach the play as part of the new Eduqas GCSE (9-1) Drama exam and other specifications. "Hard to Swallow - Easy to Digest really lives up to its namesake; Wheeller's conversational style provides an interesting, engaging and often humorous account of the creation of the play and touches on experiences that can be related to by drama students and teachers alike. Not only are key points for the new exam specifications covered, the addition of Latto's scheme of work makes exploring this thought-provoking play simple and easy. An excellent publication and a must for those teaching this play"
Adam Leigh Shea, Head of Faculty (Reading Girls' School)

It does exactly what it's says on the tin! It breaks down the text making it easy for pupils to digest, providing contextual information and ideas for lessons. The DVD has also provided my EAL pupils with a visual aid to support and deepen their understanding and provide them with some ideas for how to stage scenes.
Nike White Head of Performing Arts John Henry Newman Catholic College